Under the Editorship of
Leonard Carmichael
National Geographic Society

Houghton Mifflin Company
Boston
NEW YORK
ATLANTA
GENEVA, ILL.
DALLAS
PALO ALTO

0014820

SELF
AND
ROLE

A Theory of Self-Process and Role Behavior

John E. Horrocks
Dorothy W. Jackson
Ohio State University

Printed in the U.S.A.
Library of Congress Catalog Card Number: 76–166113
ISBN: 0–395–12641–X

Table of Contents

Editor's Foreword

This book deals with three related and central problems of present day psychology: (1) What is the self? (2) How does the self develop in each individual? (3) How is the self related to role behavior?

The authors correctly point out that today more articles on the self-concept are being published than ever before in the history of psychology. These new contributions to an understanding of this important part of mental life are reviewed in these pages in such a way as to provide a basis for the authors' own very modern synthetic view of the nature of the self and of role behavior as it is related to the self.

This new view deals with the concept of the self as a process consisting of an affective-cognitive dynamism with a structure consisting of an identity hierarchy and a value system. Readers who are familiar with the extensive literature of this field and especially with the idea of the psychogenesis of the self as developed by Jean Piaget will find an exciting new illumination in the formulation that is presented here. The separate contributions of maturation, knowledge of the external world of physical things and the experiences of the social environment are treated in a way that recognizes the interrelated importance of both cognitive processes and of evaluation.

Readers will be especially interested in the fact that the authors present a hypothetico-deductive statement of their new formulation that has been prepared so as to allow a step by step testing of their hypotheses by empirical research.

No one who reads this book can doubt that the concept, or, possibly better, the construct of the self as considered in its pages, is basic in a modern and sophisticated understanding of both the behavior and the experience of human beings at every developmental stage.

This volume is thus very modern and necessarily in part

quite technical in its language but it is written in such a clear way that it has direct significance not only for all students of general psychology but especially for those whose primary concern is with the theory and the practice of clinical psychology.

Leonard Carmichael

SELF AND ROLE

Chapter 1

The Significance of Self

MAN IS AN ORGANISM characterized by a complex and complicated state of awareness representing the culmination of eons of evolutionary development. Phylogenesis has brought him to a level of cognitive ability that enables him to conceptualize space-time relationships, and thus to be aware of his past as well as of the probable consequences of his behavior. He is able to symbolize his own experience as well as the experience of others in terms unfettered by limitations of time and space. He has a neurological-chemical apparatus enabling him to develop a capacity to learn, reason, and remember at a high order of complexity. He is able to evolve a concept of self and to consider his own nature.

Operational development of cognitive activities has come about with the acquisition of signs and symbols for specific realities existing in his world. Such realities are represented by objects and behavioral events processed from his experiences and interactions. The acquisition of language has made man a symbolizing animal capable of structuring his environments, while his needs to communicate and to act in concert with his contemporaries have made him a socialized animal capable of structuring his social interactions. With the use of signs and symbols as representations of stimulus events, he is capable of interpreting his present and past social and physical environments and can respond proactively, conceiving of and planning for future events on a contingency basis. While such interpretations and conceptions are essentially cognitive acts, they have a conative basis and usually possess

1

affective overtones. Much of his behavior is value oriented. Interpretations find expression in attitudes, opinions, verbalized positions, and statements of belief. The expression of his cognitive constructions results in approaching or avoiding behavior or in ambivalence. These resultants create resistance, assertion, permissiveness, or passivity as interactive responses to stimuli in his environment. As an interactive organism man both selectively responds to and initiates activity upon aspects of his total environment.

In the life space of any individual certain aspects of the environment are saliently significant. Such significant elements form the focus of an individual's important interpretations. They color all of his minor interpretations and hence offer clues to understanding him as a person. Some of an individual's focal points of interpretation seem universal to the culture and time in history in which he lives, but some are idiosyncratic to the individual himself.

Of all man's idiosyncratic interpretations, self-interpretation is most central to his nature. Ontogenetically, he faces the long developmental task of self-definition. He must learn to interpret and cope with himself as a functioning physical entity and to relate that entity to his physical and social environment; incoming stimuli, as well as those originating internally, must be given meaning as they are processed, organized, and integrated by cognitive processes into a representation of an individual over the course of ontogenesis. As he develops concepts of himself as an entity he simultaneously develops concepts of other entities and objects in his kaleidoscopic environment. Concepts of self, however, are products of his mental constructions and are modified through encounters with others. The effects of socialization upon his mental constructions are evidenced in his accommodations to his contemporaries and by his establishment of and existence in social organizations for interactive beneficence. Man's social and physical environments are continuous influences upon the genetic potentials of his ancestry, upon the mental constructions he creates of his own prior and present experiences with reference to himself, and upon his ability to formulate a direction for himself in terms of a future. Again and again he asks and attempts to answer "Who am I? What am I? Where am I going?" This task involves building and relating an almost infinite number of identities (symbolizations forming concepts of self) and a system of values. Such building is a gradual process occurring over a long period of time, never really ending during the life of the individual although, in its formative stages, the first two decades of life are crucial and action oriented.

During these early years, many identity concepts are not only postulated or hypothesized, they are also related to the surrounding world of persons and things and to the subjective inner world of values, goals, and needs. Each hypothesized identity concept or cluster of identity concepts has to be tested against reality through available social roles. Hypothesized identities are amenable to modification and are changed as reality proves the identity hypotheses to be inappropriate or ill-conceived. Such reality testing is a process accomplished or facilitated by actual or fantasized role behaviors. Events represented by people, things, and happenings gain meaning when they are integrated with the individual's past experiences. The culture is assimilated in the form of symbolic representation leading to patterns of adaptation integrated to the point of permitting: (a) self-dependence and other-independence; (b) an identity constellation of one's own as contrasted to the perceived identities of others; (c) conceptualization of a path into the future; (d) assumption of responsibility for self and for others; and, at the apex of the process, (e) attainment of the capacity for nonpossessive selfless love.

The dynamic process of construction of self-meaning and interpretation is the chief developmental task in the conative-affective-cognitive area of the human organism. It is also an important developmental task in the physical-physiological domain. With the development of concepts of self the organism implements its humanity as it gains a mediating process between itself and its environment. An individual's perceptions of himself are pervasive throughout his behavior. They are as much a product of emotions and motivation as they are of intellect.

A concept of self has a long history in the development of the human race. Self has been variously defined, interpreted, and explained but whatever the definition or manner of approach, the concept is ubiquitous in man's effort to understand himself. To the writers' knowledge, no language, modern or classical, primitive or sophisticated, has not included the words "I," "me," "myself," and "mine" or their equivalents. In the closing years of the last century psychologists introduced the term "self-concept" and, with their interest in clarification by means of research, have endeavored to incorporate the concept into the whole corpus of behavior and to express it in terms susceptible to verification or refutation in the daily transactions of living. As early as 1890, James in his *Principles* devoted a chapter to self; in the middle of that decade, Baldwin (1895) hypothesized a three stage development of "personal consciousness" based in part upon a child's progressive comparison of his own body with the bodies of other persons and upon his imitation of the behavior of others. Typical of this literature is Allport's (1937) developmental view that during the first years of life an individual's consciousness is devoid of self-reference, with self-consciousness developing only after the fourth or fifth year, and Lewin's (1951) contrasting point that self is a gradual formulation occurring in the second or third year with the formation of a concept of property basic to the development of self-consciousness. Indicative of the growing interest in self was the fact that in 1947, Rogers, and in 1949, Hilgard made their presidential addresses before the American Psychological Association on self-concept. Today more articles on self-concept are being published than at any previous period in the history of psychology. The concept has, of course, been a preoccupation of philosophy from the earliest days that man has attempted to come to grips with himself and with his universe.

Despite the interest of many psychologists in self-concept, other psychologists have felt that self or self-concept represents too "mentalistic" a construct for their purposes. They view self as a metaphysical concept of an order that makes it inseparable from metaphysics, hence inadmissible as a valid aspect of the science of psychology. However, clinical psychologists have found the construct useful. Wylie (1961) writes, "the clinicians may have felt less need for neat, philosophically sophisticated, operationally circumscribed theorizing. They may have been less distressed to depart from such theorizing in their search for conceptual schema to account for their observations." She further notes that "all the theories of personality which have been put forth, within the last two decades, assign importance to a phenomenal and/or non-phenomenal self-concept with cognitive and motivational attributes."

The writers' view is that the construct self is necessary for an understanding of human behavior, that it can be removed from its metaphysical status and be so hypothesized that it is a valid subject for psychological study. True, the idea of *a self* still remains largely in the realm of metaphysics, but science often progresses by attempting to take metaphysical concepts, to state them in terms of hypotheses, and then to devise research making the hypotheses susceptible to refutation. Often one has to acquire new knowledge and invent new techniques to make such a venture feasible, but the task is not necessarily impossible. Psychologists studying self should endeavor to define self so that it may be separated from its metaphysical base and anchored so that statements about self would be susceptible if not to empirical verification at least to refutation. Unfortunately, the difficulty becomes clear when one endeavors to refute the basic hypothesis, "There is a self." To observe a "self" is impossible. One can only observe an organismic entity or a manifested behavioral aspect of an entity. Obviously, then, the logical point to begin is with operational statements derived from a consideration of the developmental sequence.

During his development, a mentally intact individual learns about his own organism, as well as about his physical and social worlds, and adapts himself to his total environment. He cognitively derives ideas and beliefs providing meaning and interpretation of himself from his actual interactions and, later, by hypothetical interactions. His concepts are covertly emoted or implied and overtly manifested through interactive behavior with others. Social interaction involves participation in social exchange and conduct.

While man constructs views, attitudes, and perceptions of himself, he simultaneously derives views, attitudes, and perceptions of others. The expectations he constructs of others structure his environment and provide him patterns of behavioral response which permit a positional, status arrangement of his social world and his relationships within it. He elaborates and reorganizes his self-symbols from results of his social participations. Patterns of expected social behaviors are traditionally described as roles in a social organization. Roles are the social opportunities for expression or exemplification of self-components.

The significance of the construct self is viewed by the present writers as basic to understanding man and his behavior. While roles and self may imply a positional arrangement in an interactive system, psychological study of the constructs of self and role assumes that interaction involves behavioral responses emerging from the demands of individuals, the feedback from the person or persons with whom they are involved, and implicitly with the individual's developing cognition of the demands of the broader culture. This quality of interaction results in role behavior that may or may not be self-components manifested in situational contexts.

Since man is a social animal he structures his interactions in terms of social role adaptations; since man is a cognitively developing organism he structures his conceptualizations of self as a mental organization of his stimulus-event interactions.

By assuming self-as-process, the study of self is amenable to scientific study by focusing on the continuity of self-meanings and the changes and consistencies of the role behavioral manifestations of self over time. Stated in this manner, self is a significant developmental process occurring during the life of the human individual as he continuously attempts to define himself and his adaptation to his contemporaries.

Chapter 2

Definition of Self

MAN IS AN INTEGRAL PART of nature and must obey its physical and biological laws. His behavior and psychic being are a function of his own neurological, physiological, and chemical processes. Any definition of self violating this fundamental fact of nature is inadmissible in science. Hence, it is necessary to reject those definitions of self as a corporeal entity existing as some tangible or intangible component within the organism, and, most particularly, as an entity having an existence apart from the organism.

Self-as-Process

Self represents the continuing cognitive-affective organization and reorganization of the experienced past, experiencing of the present, and anticipated future of the organism so structured as to be symbolic of the organism's perception of its being at any point in time. Actually, self is a *process* by means of which the organism derives and constructs self-products which, taken together, represent the organism's interpretation and meaning of itself. In this relationship the organism is the entity and self is the process that evolves representations of its own entity and its related mental and behavioral activities. Operationally, defining or describing one's self is a continuously evolving product of learning, structured in the form of interacting emotional and cognitive elements. Thus, self is the *means* by which the organism is aware of and understands itself as a corporate being with a past history and a probable or possible future.

For self to be operative as a process there have to be an environmental context, a memory or storage system, continuous integration and differentiation of experiences, internal and external interaction, and feeling-affect. The development of a self-symbol has an integral relationship to the development of ability to think, thinking being an elaboration of awareness. In essence, self-process provides not only symbolizations of the organism, but also an integrally functional aspect of it. It can best be defined as a developmental construct based upon the interaction of the organism with itself, its physical environments, and its social transactions with others. It is a construct of relationships unconfined by limitations of space-time but one that can never exist apart from the neurological substrate from which it evolved.

Therefore, the position of these writers is that at any point in time self must be considered a process rather than an entity. Further, self-as-process should not be confused with its own contents, with the concepts constructed from experiences, nor with those concepts manifested as behavioral products and outcomes of social interaction. This confusion would destroy an understanding of various stages, levels, attributes, or conditions that may emerge during its development, and distort the process by equating self with an entity.

Preformation and Self

In defining self-process rejecting the idea of preformation is advisable. Of course the developing human organism has within himself a genetically coded program which guides its production as a physical organism and which, through the directional process of physical maturation and growth, is effected over the organism's life span. But at conception the psychic (mental ideational) aspect is missing and certainly has not been programmed. Dubos (1970) writes

> Experiments with laboratory animals and studies of human populations have demonstrated that biological and mental individuality reflects the influences exerted by environmental stimuli on the developing organism. In scientific jargon, this means that, contrary to what is often believed, genes do not

determine all the traits by which we know a person. What they do, rather, is to govern his biological and mental responses to the stimuli that impinge upon him. These responses become indelibly inscribed on the body and mind, thus providing patterns which impose a direction for further development.

Somatic Self *in Utero*

Self, then, is a developmental process evolving throughout the life span of a psychologically intact organism, within the parameters of that organism's physical and social environments. In the months before birth rudimentary aspects of preself-awareness may be posited. It would appear that *in utero* a developing organism may discriminate noxious from non-noxious stimuli. He can react to loud auditory sounds (Sontag and Wallace, 1935), unpleasant cutaneous stimuli, and disturbance in the uterine environment by withdrawing or attempting to "move away from" the source of stimuli. If such behavior is indicative of basic exterior-interior discrimination based on sensory perception (the process of awareness) then it appears reasonable to postulate the beginnings of somatic aspects of the self-process prior to birth. Through the process of interaction with his environment a fetus begins to formulate the anlagen, or basic rudimentary cognitive assemblies, from which the other more complex associations and patterns emerge and evolve.

Developmentally, the actions and reactions occurring *in utero* provide the neonate with some basic cognitive schema to begin coping with a new environment. Hooker (1944) and Gesell (1945) describe the newborn as continuous with his prenatal self. By repeated interactions with his environment a child builds concepts of his activity, of his mastery, and of himself in his world. To a large extent environmental stimuli activate or effect inherited potentialities which become basic elements in the individual's conceptualizations of his individuality.

Although the rudimentary structures of psychic self-awareness before birth are nebulous, there is evidence suggesting that behavioral styles and personality differences do exist among the newborn beyond those that might result from the trauma of birth or the environmental experiences provided by the first hours or days *ex utero*. Hence, such neonatal predispositions to act in a particular way are probably the result of uterine circumstances, including stress experienced by the mother; but it would appear that upon this foundation the later more structured perceptions and ideas of self are built. Despite these beginnings, however, the task of the developing organism is to build its own psychic structures during the years of its lifetime, a program limited by the physical-neurological substrate with which it has been endowed and by opportunities provided by the environment in which, initially, it is placed and in which, later, it places itself. Thus, building upon anlagen occurring before birth, the newborn begins its later emerging, more structured concepts of self. Of course the process of self-building is not accomplished by the infant alone; the social elements of his environment, including the mother or parent surrogate and other significant figures participate as well. Self-reference development may be considerably enhanced or even accelerated if the environment is made particularly favorable. It has been demonstrated, for example, that environment produces change in cognition, affect, and motivation. Therefore, by the interactive effects of the organism with his total environment, the potentials with which he was endowed may become actualized, but self-as-process is not preformed or predetermined by genetic endowment nor by environmental effects alone. Self-process is cognitive-affective processing of the experiences of the organism with his environment but is dependent upon the level of cognitive manipulation the individual has attained. The reference locus for organization of identity concepts of the self-process is the organism himself.

In the light of the foregoing discussion, a self-symbol may be further defined as a personal reference construct which involves a perceiving, interpreting, action system (i.e., possessing awareness) operating on the bases of hypotheses, images, ideas, thoughts, and expectancies formulated as the result of learning and previous experiences. Thus, concepts of self are personal, modifiable, and representative of an inner view. They involve the total construction that an observing, attending organism places upon itself and its surrounding environments—or the organism's hypotheses of the environment's past, present, and future.

Chapter 3

Origins and Elaborations
of Self

Early Developmental Origins

In ontogenetic development self-concepts are manifestations
of the development and operation of awareness as an individual encounters the task of experiencing his environment
and carving out of that experience a perception of the distinction between self and non-self. At what point in ontogenesis
does the encounter begin? There is no certain answer to this
question. Many observers hold that the zero point of encounter is birth; however, the organism *in utero* is sentient
and may be assumed to possess a form of awareness at least
analagous to that of various lower orders of phyla. Thus the
human fetus apprehends experience to the extent of possessing an undifferentiated pre-self, although the point of incep-
tion of a proto-self during embryogenesis is still unknown.
What is known is that the progress of an individual from
the fertilized egg to maturity consists of a series of epigenetic
events providing an observer with a number of different entry
points for studying the developmental sequence. Where self-
perception is concerned most psychologists typically wish to
enter after the organism is born. In doing so, however, they
should know that the organism possesses a crucial history
of awareness and of apprehension of experience starting before their point of entry. A complete examination of the

genesis of self should certainly give some consideration to the possibility of embryological origins.

The position of the present writers is that during the course of embryological development the human organism, following its genetic program, becomes a functional physical and physiological stimulus-response system. The system is characterized by awareness and becomes capable, before birth, of somatic perception leading to its apprehension of an undifferentiated pre-self. At birth the organism enters a new physical environment offering its stimulus-response system a whole sequence of new experiences. In its new environment the developing physical system begins to program into itself expectancies, sets, and directionality, providing the rudimentary beginnings of a perception of a personal physical entity or a somatic self. Almost simultaneously the presence of other persons begins to provide culturally engendered experiences. The action is still focused on the body recognition and manipulation aspect, and although the infant begins to learn to respond to significant others as functionally facilitative, there are as yet no beginnings of an ideational self-percept.

The first task in the building of a somatic self-percept involves the organism's gradual awareness of himself as an entity, separate from his immediately surrounding and changing environment. He then has the task of locating, differentiating, manipulating, and controlling its component parts and of developing responses and coordinations leading to the control and manipulation of the environment to serve his own directionality and stimulus hunger. Through these interactions the somatic percept becomes well formulated and the infant arrives at a state in which he can distinguish the major external parts of his body from his surrounding environment. He is able to move the various parts of his body without any expectation that everything in his immediate vicinity will also move. In short, he is functionally autonomous in fact as well as in expectation.

Basic Drives

Underlying and governing growth and development is the presence of basic drives, some characteristic of all matter and some characteristic primarily of organisms that have evolved to the level of complexity represented by the human infant. Throughout the life span of the organism, as maturation, learning, and experience add complexity, the basic drives remain compelling forces in originating and guiding behavior.

What are the fundamental drives of life and of the human organism? The answer to this question has been of perennial interest to psychologists and biologists as well as philosophers. Various lists of fundamental impulsions to behavior have been formulated and drives categorized as innate or acquired, learned or unlearned. Usually, however, one or more drives have been selected as primary. In fact, various theorists have built whole systems of behavior around the assumption that a single drive is the root of all behavior. Among these Freud proposed the primacy of the libido, Adler that of inferiority-power, Frankl the drive for meaning, and Russell the quest for power. Common to all is the assumption of their motivational influence and the postulation that they represent ends toward which the organism is striving or inherently propelled. But such formulations can only be hypotheses representing inferences from observed or conjectured behavior. They lack scientific proof or even, at the present state of knowledge, the possibility of scientific proof. Their value is that they are heuristic, serving to offer a hypothetical explanation for the appearance of behavioral phenomena, or to aid in prediction and therapeutic application.

The present writers propose four fundamental life drives and one drive characteristic primarily of the human organism which they offer as tenable assumptions based upon hypothesis and observation of behavioral phenomena. The four basic drives are organization, completion, motility, and equilibrium. The human organism drive is that of synthesis-integration. The writers postulate these drives as primary in the human organism and see them as governing principles basic to all its behavior. Hence, the five drives are postulated as essential guiding forces in the development of self-process and its products. In the living human organism the manifestations of the five drives are not unrelated, forming rather a complementary whole in the processes of development and behavior.

The Organization Principle

Man is a biological organism and to that extent there can be no doubt that the operation of every component part of the organism could be reduced to the mechanistic base of process or makeup expressible in terms of chemistry or physics. But, as Von Bertalanffy (1933, 1952) notes, there is something more. While one may reject the idea of vitalistic purposiveness it is still impossible to explain the wholeness of the organism in terms of physics and chemistry. It would appear that the something more, the element that holds the organism together as a functioning unit, is the fact of organization. The very life of the organism as an entity depends upon the maintenance of the reciprocal relationship of its components. Organization itself depends upon two factors. One is cohesion and the other reciprocity. The writers take the position that maintenance of intra-organismic organization is one of the four[1] basic drives of a living organism at any level of evolutionary development.

Some theorists have postulated maintenance of life as a fundamental drive, but that would appear to be an outcome of the organization principle and simply represents a teleological interpretation of purposiveness. In a developing organism one can always expect to find functional evidences of the drive for organization representing functional intactness[2] long before, in its human form, it has symbols or a self-percept enabling it to express the drive in any way other than gross actions and responses. With the appearance of a self-percept and the capacity to symbolize, the observer may find many socialized and personalized examples of the organization drive in an individual's need-directed behavior. However, the area of the internal cognitive processes involving meaning

[1] The fifth drive, synthesis-integration, is not an attribute of all living organisms.

[2] Reproduction by division, as in amoeba, finds an organism apparently yielding its original intactness, but the members of the resulting pair are each a functionally intact whole. In certain areas of pathology, such as cancer, the organism embarks on a course of development that will eventually destroy it, but the anomalous growth, once underway, follows a lawful biological course of development as a part of the organism's wholeness. The course of such anomalous development results from the operation of the completion principle.

relationships is where the most crucial application of the organization principle to self-process will be found.

Equilibrium

Equilibrium, a fundamental life drive, is a stable condition within the organism in which opposing tensions, forces, and processes are balanced so that a constancy of relations is maintained. The attainment and maintenance of equilibrium is essential to the continuation of life. Over a hundred years ago Claude Bernard spoke of the need for a stable *milieu interne*. Nearly a half century ago Rignano (1923) wrote

> Every organism is a physiological system in a stationary condition and tends to preserve this condition or to restore it as soon as it is disturbed by any variation occurring within or outside the organism. This property constitutes the foundation and essence of all "needs," of all "desires," of all the most important appetites. All movements of approach or withdrawal, of attack or flight, of seizing of rejecting which animals make are only so many direct or indirect consequences of this very general tendency of every stationary physiological condition to remain constant.

Cannon's research (1932) on equilibrium focused on the lack of effect of changing environments on the constancy of internal physicochemical states. He wrote

> The constant conditions which are maintained in the body might be termed *equilibria*. That word, however, has come to have fairly exact meaning as applied to relatively simple physicochemical states, in closed systems, where known forces are balanced. The coordinated physiological processes which maintain most of the steady states in the organism are so complex and so peculiar to living beings—involving, as they may, the brain and nerves, the heart, lungs, kidneys and spleen, all working cooperatively—that I have suggested a special designation for these states, *homeostasis*. The word does not imply something set and immobile, a stagnation. It means a condition—a condition which may vary, but which is relatively constant.

These writers agree with Cannon's comprehensive view of the homeostatic condition but wish to retain what they feel is the more dynamic term, equilibrium, applying it to open as well as to closed systems. They propose, therefore, the specific extension of the concept of equilibrium to the neurological and perceptual processes comprising cognition.[3] In this way equilibrium is a fundamental life drive characteristic of the whole organism and is essential to the formation of self-concepts.

The Completion Principle

The third basic drive of the human organism, also characteristic of all living forms and closely associated with the organization principle, is the drive for order and completion. In nature as in mathematics and music, there is order, and part of the order is for a note, a mathematical equation, and an event in nature to run its course. For living organisms this sequence represents a developmental principle of completion in terms of the structural pattern that evolution in its selection of efficiency has laid down for any given organism. The completion principle provides directionality to behavior in the sense of forward thrust, continuance, and non-reversibility. Through the process of completion an organism attains and maintains equilibrium.

The drive for completion explains the genetically programmed course of embryological development leading to the completed organism *ex utero*. It also explains the force of the surge of development and growth which will lead an organism to destroy itself in order to fulfill its developmental destiny. For example, a starving child will continue to grow and in effect will kill himself as a result of the growth his diet cannot sustain.

The Principle of Motility-Unrest

Accompanying the drives for maintenance of organization, for attainment and maintenance of equilibrium, and for com-

[3] In his complacency theory of motivation Raup (1925) uses the term equilibrium noting that it is the most fundamental principle of all life processes as well as of behavior. He extends equilibrium to include behavioral adjustment of the organism in its environment. For Raup, maladjustment represents a disturbance of balance between an organism and its environment. Maladjustment activates the drive to restore equilibrium (complacency).

pletion is a basic state of unrest which takes the form of motility, historically known as conation, which drives the organism forward, placing it in a state of "becoming." In phylogenesis conation is the antecedent of organization and completion for it represents the continual motion that is not only an attribute of all living matter but that, at the molecular level, is characteristic of inorganic matter as well. Sperry (1952) and others hold that aware life originated in motion and that motion continues to be the very essence of life. For that reason motility should be added to organization, completion, and equilibrium to provide a primary level of drives basic to any individual's development of self-percepts in that they must inevitably condition as well as limit factors in such development.

Synthesis-Integration as a Drive

Of particular importance in the development of self-percept is the existence of a basic cognitive drive for synthesis-integration growing out of the phylogenetically evolved neurological structure of man. Synthesis-integration presupposes a relatively complex cognitive structure capable of processing and interpreting exterior experience and internal sensation. The cognitive structure is accompanied by the cognitive capacity to find meaningful relationships and integrate these with the whole matrix of past experience, present interactions, and with the expectation of future experience. For that reason the possession of a drive to accomplish synthesis-integration can only be an attribute of an advanced cognizing organism such as man. Unlike the drives for organization, completion, equilibrium, and motility the synthesis-integration drive does not appear until late in the evolutionary sequence.

Synthesis-integration represents a drive to utilize retained cognitive products and to create new meaning relationships. The life history of the functioning human organism consists of a continual endeavor to attribute meaning to the stimuli with which it is presented. This occurs by a process of relating new stimuli to previously acquired stimuli. In this sense, when confronted by a new stimulus event man is driven to find a locus for the event within his universe of experiences. Meaning derives from the location and processing of a stimulus event.[4] Thus, synthesis-integration may be explicated as a drive to find meaning and to experience closure when the human organism is confronted by the inputs from interior and exterior sources with which he is continually bombarded.

A conditional factor on the operation of the synthesis-integration drive is the functional demand of the equilibrium drive that synthesis will eventuate in a state in accord with the self-concepts an individual has developed to that point as well as with his world concepts. The latter concepts represent his view of how things are in his immediate environment and in his geographically removed environment.

Organ Tensions

In addition to the five primary drives a group of impulsions to behavior is also based upon the functioning of an organ or a group of organs having a specific physiological task in the internal economy of the body. They represent simple physiological tension states characterized by sensations accompanying localized muscular activity and strain. As with all tension states they place the organism in a condition marked by uneasiness or unrest and by pressure and readiness to act. Some of these, such as sexual tension, can become more intricately elaborated and socialized in their expressions than is true of others, thus becoming the starting point for the building of a whole constellation of goals and social behaviors related to evolved self-concepts. In their pure physiological state, while such organ tensions do lead to action they do not have the status of drives represented by the all-pervasive fundamental drives described in the foregoing discussions. The four fundamental life drives operate in all phases of behavior, whereas the spheres of activity of the organ are more limited. The fundamental drives, including synthesis-integration, act in guiding the social behavioral elaborations as well as the actual physical functioning resulting from organ tensions.

---

[4] Meaning is further defined in Chapter 6 and the problem of meaning loci is made explicit in the discussion accompanying the definition.

Psychological Needs

In addition to the fundamental drives and organ tensions, the developing human organism evolves through learning various impulsions to behavior, termed needs, to be considered in understanding the development of his self-concepts. A need may be defined as a condition, activity, or thing whose attainment is evaluated by an individual as personally satisfying or facilitative, or as promoting the welfare of himself and his concerns. The condition or activity may be internal or external, and the evaluation may or may not be made at the conscious level. Evaluation leading to need assumption is a cognitive-affective act and hence is conditioned by an individual's experience and level of development. Needs, once present, create in the individual a behavioral agenda which is usually implemented by the roles he attempts either in actuality or in imagination. It is the implementation of this agenda which provides the observer with an index to an individual's percepts of himself.

In considering needs it must be understood that they are evaluative derivations, at various levels of importance, from the base of the organ tensions and the five fundamental drives. Further, they tend to be resultants of the organism's evolved structure. In a real sense the psychological needs represent personalized and socialized extensions and elaborations of drives and organ tensions. An individual's construction of his psychological needs is conditioned by the parameters and directions set by his fundamental drives.

Needs are learned. Before their appearance in any human individual there is only a living organism possessing drives and organ tensions, developing in accordance with its genetic program. Needs are learned and develop as the organism encounters experience and begins to attribute meaning to internal and external stimuli. The impact of others, through socialization, is a major force shaping the individual. Many of his needs arise from his social encounters as well as from his own internal self and organ demands. Their behavioral outcomes are an individual's acceptance of goals toward which to strive, the goals representing various needs socialized and elaborated through learning and experience. Need-goal behavior can become simple habituated response.[5] While need behavior is usually thought of as overt positive performance, negation or inhibition of behavior may be a need resultant.

Since needs develop as a result of experience and learning on the part of a specific individual it is inevitable that in his particular cognitive-affective system some needs will assume primacy. The result is a hierarchy of needs, the hierarchy being built on the demand value of each need and its generality across various personal, social, and environmental situations. Some needs tend to be situation specific, and no matter how strong their demand in that situation, or in similar situations, the need appears to be inoperative in others.

Since needs result from specific learning and social experience, needs and their hierarchical arrangement will tend to be peculiar to each individual. However, some needs, due to ubiquitous cultural expectations and the human structure, will be quite universal and high in the hierarchy of all individuals in a given culture. Of these, manipulation-mastery is a particularly good example. In broad outline one can start with the apparatus the newborn organism brings into the world and start with "reflexes." Take, for example, the sucking reflex, characteristic of most newborn individuals, which inevitably leads to ingestion and to mastery of a portion of the exterior world in the sense that the neonate encompasses it or takes it into himself.[6] But, in addition to the sucking reflex the neonate is endowed with all kinds of structural equipment which allows him to manipulate his environment and thus to master it. Function is related to structure and when an organism whose structure makes manipulation possible is placed in a situation where manipulation can occur it will occur. Given an opposable thumb it is inevitable that it will be used sooner or later, the extensions of its use being

---

[5] Habit represents an individual's tendency to react in a certain way when confronted by a stimulus. The strength of the habit is expressed in terms of the likelihood of its occurrence when the organism is confronted with a stimulus.

[6] It is recognized that the sucking "reflex" is adaptive. The neonate learns to use it to best suit himself. There are different styles even in the basic behavior patterns.

dictated by drives and needs and their elaborations.[7] Mastery occurrences happen at first by chance due to the motility-unrest drive of the organism but are later elaborated as a result of conditioning, experience, and the process of socialization. Ambition for vocational success may represent one extension of the mastery need. A need for power is a derivation of mastery although it may also have further cognitive and need elements. Needs can grow out of, or be derived from, other needs.

The fact of need impulsions to behavior is widely accepted in psychological theory, and numerous lists of needs have been formulated. For example, Buytendik (1958) speaks of security, Frankl (1959) of the quest for meaning in life, Krakovskii (1962) of the concern for self-assertion, and Buhler (1958) of patterns of mastery-adaptation and activity-passivity. Murray (1938) presents a list of twenty-eight "secondary" needs, and Maslow (1954) lists safety needs, belonging and love needs, esteem needs, need for self-actualization, desires to know and understand, and esthetic needs. Such listings of needs have value in studying the behavioral manifestations of self-concept; but, from a developmental point of view a common mistake has been to try to list basic needs without operational reference to the structure, drives, and life processes of the organism. A confusing tendency has been to assign fundamental drive status to needs and to ignore the fact that they are the products of structural function and of specific experiences and socialization.[8]

Tension and Affect

Tension is energy for a drive or need state caused by blocking any of the five basic drives, psychological needs, or organ functions. During a state of tension the organism's condition

[7] Structure requires functioning to develop further the structure to realize its potential. The functioning of a structure results in mastery of its functioning effects observed as environmental manipulation.

[8] The present writers have made no attempt to postulate a list of psychological needs for this volume. Possibilities for inclusion are almost unlimited, and their presentation in a theory of self-process would serve no useful purpose.

is that of uneasiness, restless activity, and readiness to act. In general terms tension represents a state of energy resulting in activity leading to the possibility of tension reduction. Tension may exist as either an emotional or a physiological condition although either may give rise to the other.

Tension constitutes the affective aspect of behavior and is a conditioning factor in the operation of the organism's cognitive processes. The form of behavior resulting from tension usually follows habituated patterns resulting from past experiences and represents an individual's cognitive-affective styles. In some individuals tension induced behavior follows adjustive patterns, while in others it is characteristically non-adjustive.

From the point of view of self-concept theory the cognitive aspects of tension are seen by the writers as functionally important in self-process and self-concept formation. When an aspect of the environment becomes a stimulus event by entering an individual's field of awareness it becomes a cognitive irritant leading to activation of the cognitive process. Initially, there is a lack of closure (completion) of varying duration depending upon the familiarity of the stimulus as the result of previous attributions of meaning.[9] When closure is incomplete or in process, integration is impossible and the individual remains in a state of tension until closure or some acceptable solution is arrived at. For any given situation the intensity of tension, and hence of affect, that lack of closure induces is partly a function of an individual's values (or when he is younger, his collection of rules) as well as of his previous experiences.

Stimulus events may be either molar or molecular, and they may originate either within or outside the organism. A letter of the alphabet is a molecular external stimulus. A need represents a molar or more complicated internal stimulus, but the organism's cognitive need-stimulus behavior is similar to that occurring in the case of a molecular stimulus. An organism blocked in the consummation of its drive or need behavior or in the progress of its genetic program is in a state

---

[9] A stimulus is familiar if it possesses, as a result of previous exposure, a meaning location in an individual's experiential universe. If it is new it is unfamiliar and meaningless until it or aspects of it are assessed and assigned a meaning location.

of tension. The intensity of the tension is a function both of the importance to the organism of the goals blocked and in the amount of progress made in their attainment.

Development of Reactivity

During his first months of life a newborn infant is exposed to a multitude of novel experiences comprising the vast "buzzing confusion" that is his world. Some of the experiences are repeated again and again until they grow familiar and meaningful. Gradually confusion begins to yield to order. During this early period, as has been previously indicated, the new individual's basic drives, as well as the consequences of his organ tension states, find elaboration in the form of psychological needs. Such needs are directly related to the individual's development of body-percepts and of a concept of a somatic self. They are reinforced and rewarded through primary socialization involving imitation and identification with the agents of his personal social interactions.

As new needs are met an elaboration occurs within the cognitive-affective processing system inter-relating associations, actions, and experiences, and integrating the affectivity engendered by interactions with the environment. In response to its drives and needs the organism receives environmental feedback about its competence or effectiveness in its attempts to meet its organ demands. The infant is not only an *active* organism, it is also a *reactive* one in interaction with the environment; these activity modes result in the development and elaboration of cognitive-affective structures from which evolve the percepts and concepts of somatic and psychic self.

Groundwork for Self-Percept

Given that the fetus reacts to noxious stimuli or uterine influences with some behavioral response, it follows that the genesis of awareness based on discrimination or affectivity is part of the first cognitive structures. It appears possible that the primary cognitions depend upon discrimination of, or reaction to, stimuli based upon sensory affect. However, sensory affect is an action-reaction to an immediate environmental event. It is not interpreted as "good" or "bad" because such evaluation depends upon the establishment of prior criteria or the classification of prior experiences into some patterned cognitive organization. At the earliest levels of awareness rudimentary cognitions are the result of total organismic responses. These responses are global or diffuse behavioral activities resulting from exposure to stimuli. Repetitions of stimuli will develop a response pattern or memory storage of events. These initiation responses are the ways an organism initially responds to stimuli and are fundamental to learning.

Attending may be viewed as a selective motivational action on the part of the organism. When an organism acts upon environmental stimuli it begins to develop rudiments (anlagen) of cognitive functions. Affect develops from and is inherent in the results of feedback received and processed by the organism from its action and the effects of its action on its environment. Affect is an integral aspect of the anlagen of cognitive structure being formed.

Somatic Origins of Self-Process

A concept of somatic self leads to the establishment of lower level value concepts based on the worth and goodness or badness of objects, people, and situations. In its area of application the somatic self-concept provides criteria for judgment of meaningful stimuli and becomes a standard providing a determination of behavior.

A somatic self-concept is formulated with a specific biological reference. At the point when an infant has begun to know what he is, he has made a beginning toward the construction of a self based on ideation and mentation. He has taken the first steps beyond the gross bodily perception characteristic of the prenatal and neonatal period. Gradually a change is effected as the motivating force for the psychological needs, referred to as desires or wants, becomes increasingly important. However, the organ tension demands, while still requiring reduction, are supplied and given interpretations in a form having implications far beyond that of simple organ tissue tension reduction.

The fact that one's own body is always an important element in the development of self-concepts may be observed in an infant. One of his tasks is to separate his own body from his surroundings and recognize it and its parts as his. Once the body is closely defined as part of oneself it remains a source of interest and exploration throughout childhood and into adolescence. This interest is perfectly natural and is in no sense morbid. It is simply part of growing up and recognizing oneself as oneself. If the child grows up in an environment in which physical things such as strength, endurance, appearance, or health are held to be important, then interest in the body will be even greater.[10]

Sherif and Cantril (1947) noted that "the adolescent's already accentuated awareness and focusing on his body becomes even more acute with more pronounced, somewhat stylized attention of others (for example, parents and other adolescents) on his or her body, with sex desires toward and from age mates now present in a developed way." Such accentuation of the adolescent's interest in bodily things may take several forms, among them an increased interest in the opposite sex, in personal appearance and development, in strength and endurance, and in personal health.

With such changes of interest in the physical aspects of sex, youths not only become interested in the physical pres-

[10] It is characteristic of human beings to have a concept of physical self, including a body image. The idea of a body image, developed by Schilder (1950) and elaborated by Kolb (1959) and Schonfeld (1963), posits the body image as evolving from internalized psychological factors, cultural influences, concepts of the ideal body denoting cultural or universal stereotypes and an individual's personal perception of his body appearance and its functional ability. Zachry and Lighty (1940) put the matter well when they speak of the body as a "symbol of the self." When physical changes or additions occur which require radical revisions in one's physical self-concept, it is usually difficult to adjust to the new physical actuality as well as to the new physical self-concept that actuality involves. An adult who finds himself putting on weight, balding, losing youthful good looks, or accumulating physical disabilities is in somewhat the same situation as the adolescent who is also undergoing physical changes which appear to be out of control. Perhaps it is more difficult for an adolescent to adjust to physical change than for an adult because an adolescent tends to be less prepared for the changes or less able to recognize their factual meaning. An additional factor is that the adolescent's values may be such that he overestimates the importance of physical things and is less willing to accept changes.

ence of others, but think of their own bodies from the viewpoint of others who may observe them. There is a change from an egocentric preoccupation with one's body for its own sake, to a preoccupation with one's own body as it relates to others. Motives are often mixed in a given individual, or they may vary from individual to individual. The adolescent has conflicting desires. On the one hand, he wants to look well, to attract, to display; on the other, he wants to hide those physical attributes of which he is ashamed. The latter attitude is, of course, built upon misunderstanding, but it is real enough when it exists. It is, in fact, a cognitive process of forming concepts of one's body image based on prior experiences of self with others. Affectivity becomes encoded into the cognitive structures resulting from interactions. Zachry and Lighty (1940) write of a girl who enveloped herself in a "voluminous smock" because she was "larger and heavier than her contemporaries" and desired only to hide. Many a girl whose breasts are beginning to develop refuses to stand erect when asked to recite in front of her class; she slouches or slumps so that she will be less "revealing." Other girls glory in their physical changes and go to extreme lengths in wearing tight clothing and other attention-attracting devices to parade their new maturity. Both attitudes are unhealthy or at least the result of misconception, and they may be attributed to faulty education about the true meaning of physical change.

But sex is only one aspect of physical concepts of self. Some preoccupations with appearance and body functions occur for reasons of sex attraction, but sometimes for other reasons, one of the most common of which is to appear well and to stand revealed to others in accordance with one's self-concept. Physical preoccupation may be highly exaggerated. If the actuality departs too far from an ideal concept, a person may make intense efforts to alter reality. If improvement fails, then the next step may be pronounced feelings of insecurity, inferiority, and anxiety.

Ideational Origins of Self-Process

One of the most dramatic demarcation lines in the development of the self is when the human organism becomes capable of symbolization, leading to all the complexities of language. This ability is rudimentary at first but gradually what may be called cognitive self-constructions ("I want . . . ," "Give me . . . ," "I won't . . .") grow. In the early stages of symbolization percepts of somatic self and cognized abstractions of self are not really distinguished by the organism. The analogy is the child's difficulty at birth in separating himself from his surroundings.

But the separation continues and there is now a duality, related but separate, of conceptual systems. One system involves cognitive constructions of self, the other involves somatic perceptions of self. The two self-systems are often in conflict. Their integration into a combined self-meaning is both the task of normal development and a major source of neuroses, psychoses, problem behavior, and maladjustment.

By the time the basic needs have socialized and elaborated and as the individual symbolizes and distinguishes between his somatic and ideational self, it is possible to postulate a concept of purposive behavior. Such behavior is based on directionality engendered by the organism's cognitive-affective process for decision making. This process integrates and organizes self-concepts, creating values for setting standards and criteria for the organism and its interactions with others.[11]

Exteriorization

In the early stages of development an individual's self-concepts are diffuse to the point of being amorphous. Following an individual's self-localization as a physical entity is the problem of his relationship with others. The development of self-concepts proceed under conditions of social interchange. Just as an individual must build a conception of himself so must he build a conception of others and somehow arrive at a working relationship between these conceptions. Normally developing individual's somatic self-other distinctions are made without difficulty, but in the psychic realm of who and what one is the distinctions may at first be somewhat blurred. During this

---

[11] A discussion of value formation and the relationship of values to the self-process will be found in Chapter 7.

period individuals tend to extend their self-boundaries by a form of psychological exteriorization. Exteriorization represents a psychological extension of oneself outside one's own physical entity in the sense of engulfing other persons and even nonhuman objects as part of the self-system. Such exteriorization is incompatible with integrated, consistent self-cognitions and is resisted with increasing age and additional experiences. In his resistance the individual typically becomes egocentric in not extending self-integration to others. This leads to the negativistic phases of early childhood and middle adolescence. In the young child, as cognitions representing self become less diffuse—that is, with the appearance of some self-integration and self-security—there is a tendency to return to exteriorization for additional inputs concerning the individual's personal limits and references. In middle adolescence, faced with possible self-reintegration and the self-insecurity of revising and testing of self-concepts against reality there tends to be an abandoning of exteriorization and a resumption of the defensive stance of negativism. Late adolescence and maturity, with their greater self-security engendered by an integrated and tested self-view, permit a resumption of exteriorization, but at that time it is of a different order, taking the form of affiliation or love.

In its earlier stages during childhood exteriorization may simply be an extension to the other person as a manipulative device enabling the individual to implement his self-concept outside his own physical boundaries. "My teddy bear is me— when you spank me it hurts him."[12] Later the exteriorization is more a matter of "giving away" as a synthesis integration of self to another. In reality it becomes a "selfless" reaction. The capacity for such exteriorization has been postulated to represent true maturity.

Self-Indulgence and Exemplification

In considering the developmental progression of the self two important self-motivations may be postulated. One is the

---

[12] The teddy bear or any toy, object, or figmented thing, is an extention of himself outside of his own corporeal limits. He becomes capable of talking to himself, manipulating himself, punishing, and loving himself by his actions upon the exteriorized self-object.

exemplification and perpetuation of idealized concepts of self. When an individual is old enough to learn the moral criteria and ideal expectations of a general culture as well as of the various subcultures in which he lives, he tends to make personal evaluations in these ideal terms. He learns what is considered good and bad and avoids dissonance by assuming a self-view exemplifying cultural values and expectations. Thus, there is a well defined tendency for nearly everyone to attempt a self-view allowing self-interpretation in the best possible light—the "good," the "unselfish" person, "the white knight in shining armor." Despite evidence to the contrary this exemplary view is normally interpreted by an individual as his real self—a version he feels would find universal approval if only others could see it too. Working toward realization of this idealization represents self-exemplification. Of the self-exemplary behaviors altruism[13] and selfless love represent examples of the most mature level.

The second motivation is that of self-indulgence. Self-indulgence focuses upon those hedonic aspects of behavior catering to physical appetites, "creature" comforts, pleasure, and self-aggrandizement. In their more epicurean form self-indulgent behaviors may meet with certain kinds of social approval, as in the case of the gourmet or the pleasure-seeker whose activities are in accord with those of others of like inclination.

Developmentally hedonic needs appear earlier than self-exemplary needs since the latter require time for the interactions of socialization to become encoded into the cognitive-affective structures to form the basis for conceptualized values. But the transition from a major focus on tissue needs (requirements for preservation and maintenance of existence) to self needs (wants and desires for establishing a perpetuation, a pattern, and directionality for living) provide a conflict and throughout life there is a fluctuation as these need areas strive to gain the ascendency. Here in this conflict area we find the basis of neuroses and psychoses. This same conflict forms the *raison d'être* of the mental mechanisms which form

---

[13] Altruism is self-exemplary behavior which is derived from intrinsically motivated self-other responsibility. See Chapter 11 for discussion of responsibility.

our self-defenses. But developmentally the socialization battle is lost, as in late old age and in senescence, first the hedonic needs and eventually the organ tension relief needs regain ascendency and the circle is complete. In old age the self-view becomes increasingly constricted and its horizons more and more those of the body functions and their satisfaction. Figure 1 presents a schematic view of the ontogenetic progression of needs in the human organism.

Thus, very early in development the organ tensions and their derived needs are primary with goals representing objects for satisfaction of somatic needs. Later in development the rules an individual understands and employs and, even later, the values to which he adheres, change and modify his self-behaviors. The goals to which he aspires are the objectification of the needs, evidenced as behavioral directions his

FIGURE 1   Progression of Needs Over Life Span

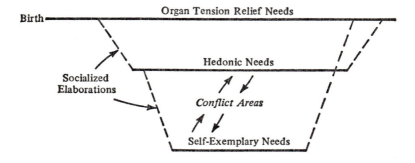

values have created. Thus, values become primary in psychic life modifying concepts of self and their exemplification in role behavior.

Considering the development of an individual's concepts of self, three questions are particularly crucial: (a) what determines the values to which he adheres; (b) how is it possible to evaluate a successful realization of a particular value; and (c) how do values change and modify the structuring of an individual's behavior?

Initially the basic micro-social unit, his family, and later the broader culture ascribe values that become processed and assessed as self-standards of an individual. If a person grows up in a society that values honesty, obedience, cleanliness, abstinence, etc., then these values, if assimilated or encoded into the cognitive-affective processing system, become rules or standards for that person's behavior and the criteria for self-evaluation and self-reference. The individual builds his concepts of identity in terms of these values and evaluates himself in terms of their successful fulfillment. His choice of roles objectifies the needs or behavioral directions created by these values. Values form the basis and source of self-evaluation of an identity hierarchy. Therefore, goals as roles realistically or hypothetically performed are directly related to an individual's self-exemplary behavior styles and to a value system which determines his self-reference, self-evaluation, behavioral directions and identity concepts.

Overview

As a result of the developmental process each individual evolves personal self-symbols involving both a somatic and a cognitive self. One problem of development is that the definition and meaning of the personal self rests upon two opposed concepts. The ideal self is based on the individual's value system and the operational self is derived from reality testing of hypothesized identities in keeping with perceived situational demands. An individual also evolves a concept of his environment based upon experience as well as a concept based upon supposition. Both these environmental concepts may be described in general terms, although within the parameters of each are various subclasses and deviations. However, where personal concepts of self are concerned, most normally developing persons tend to visualize themselves in terms of the self-exemplary behaviors which are cognitively-affectively determined through their personal value systems.

Chapter 4

Cognitive Function

Cognitive Activation

Cognition is a general term for those processes by which an organism apprehends and imparts meaning to a stimulus object or idea or a grouping of objects or ideas. Early in his developmental sequence, starting even before he is born, a human individual inhabits an environment exposing him to the possibility of cognitive activation by an almost infinite number of stimulus possibilities, some external to himself as an organism, others representing his own internal functioning and its products. Many, perhaps most, possible stimuli are not perceived by the individual and, hence, do not enter his field of awareness. When an aspect of the environment, because of previous learnings and attributions of meaning, because of its perceived relationship to the individual's drive-need system, or because of its attention demanding quality, does enter or become part of his field of awareness, it becomes for him an actual stimulus leading to the possibility of response. However, even when a stimulus does enter an individual's field of awareness leading to some preliminary response set, it may not become the object of specific focused attention. When the stimulus does become the object of specific attention or effects the use of a perceptual mode of responding, it becomes for the individual a stimulus event. Such stimulus events are cognitively processed by the individual at a level of complexity consonant with his attained stage of development.[1] As a result of cognitive processes, each new stimulus event takes on meaning and becomes a contributor to his universe of meanings. A universe of meanings is a cognitive organization of prior experiences reintegrated and interrelated to impart meaning or interpretation to stimulus cues. It operates as the individual's reference system for the interpretation of his internal and external environments. As an individual proceeds through life he is exposed to and cognitively processes a continuous kaleidoscope of stimulus events. Hence, he is capable of deriving new interpretations from prior experiences by interrelating them with present stimulus cues.

Nature of Cognition

Cognition involves, among other things, perceiving, recognizing, conceiving, relating, judging, and reasoning. In cognitive process the complex of imprints of past experience upon the organismic structure are combined with the attributes of the presented stimulus object or situational event to determine how that object or event will be perceived and processed. The expectancies and assumptions that an individual makes about his internal and external world are outcomes of the cognitive process. The manner in which he sees and interrelates the various aspects of his entire environment define an individual's cognitive structures. Obviously, cognition, conation, and affection are inseparable interrelated components of the behavior of the perceiving-interpreting human organism.

Since concepts of self may be viewed as perceptual-interpretive dynamisms, it is reasonable to assume that development of self must proceed within the parameters of what is happening to the individual over time, and that elements of cognitive function must be incorporated into a theory dealing with the processes of self. Obviously, an organism can do no more than it is cognitively capable of doing. The organism's cognitive structures and operational activity are both facilitating and limiting factors in the implementation of its conceptuali-

[1] The discussion concerning stimuli, attending, loci and meaning are further elaborated upon and presented in Chapter 6.

zations. In discussing a perceiving-interpreting action system, one immediately places the process of awareness of self within the individual through his cognitive organization of interactions with his environment conditioned by affective feedback.

Theoretical Approaches in Cognition

Various theory-based approaches are designed to furnish an understanding of cognitive development as it is manifested within an organism. One way to consider cognitive behavior is as a form of internal mapping or of a network of implicit responses. Still another approach would examine the strategies by which an individual arrives at various levels of decision by a selective collection of inputs. Festinger (1957) discusses the individual's adoption of particular strategies; Heider (1958) speaks of perception of a significant environment and the achievement of structure or cognitive balance; Gardner (1962, 1964), of control structure; Kagan et al. (1963), of conceptual strategies; and Witkin (1964), of cognitive styles. Cross (1967) defines development as "a progression along a continuum of conceptual simplicity to complexity."

Harvey, Hunt, and Schroder (1961) write that the individual's conceptual system is an "experiential filter through which impinging events are screened, gauged, and evaluated; a process that determines in large part what responses can and will occur." An individual builds a conceptual system and through it he interprets his world; the process of building and the acts of interpreting fall into a mutually reinforcing relationship in the sequence of time over which that individual develops. The developmental issue here is the level of cognitive manipulation available in building his system. Obviously, if he is unable to formulate hypotheses or to manipulate space-time relationships, his cognitive view will be limited and, in effect, less formal.[2] As an individual grows older his movement is toward greater abstractive behavior, "as progressive development occurs, a person orders his world more realistically . . . he operates more in terms of multiple alternatives

---

[2] Emphasis upon form or rules at the expense of matter or content, e.g., formal logic dealing with rules that define validity in thinking.

rather than in terms of bifurcated black-white categories."
Harvey, Hunt, and Schroder (1961) relate cognitive and personality development in a system comprising the four developmental levels: unilateral dependence, negative independence,
mutuality, and mutuality and autonomy, with various transitional stages occurring as the individual progresses from one
of the four levels to the next. In terms of developmental sequence the first level, unilateral dependence, is characterized
by external control and acceptance of absolutes from externally derived controls. The second level, negative independence, is characterized by the beginnings of internal control and
resistance to completely external authoritarian control. The
third level, mutuality, is one in which other persons are
viewed less subjectively, in terms of others' standards, with
the result that mutual relationships are possible and alternative views may be held simultaneously. During the fourth
level, mutuality and autonomy are integrated, and functioning is characterized by abstract standards, the availability of
alternative conceptual schema, and the ability to hold a strong
view without distorting incoming information. Progression
through these levels is paced by maturation of the organism
and the appearance of new environmental demands.

In their configurational discussions the Gestalt psychologists
have advanced a theory of cognitive development involving an
assumption that successive experiences leave "traces" in neural structures, so that later responses in a temporal sequence
are the result not only of the immediate situation confronting
the organism but also of the remaining traces of previous experience. With increasing age, an individual can be expected
to superimpose an increasing succession of learnings upon the
advances of the maturational components of growth. In doing
so, he builds up a vast accumulation of available memory
traces which he can use in new situations and thus he becomes capable of an increasing number of complex responses.
Thus, Gestalt psychologists conceive of cognitive development
primarily as learning and, at least in the younger days of the
organism, as sensorimotor behavior maturation. Theirs is not
a stage theory since it depends upon a continuous accretion
of experience over time with no specific or dramatic lines of
demarcation, and since it does not refer to emergence of a

qualitatively new form of thinking not evidenced in prior levels of development. Experience, rather than age, was the critical factor.[3]

Others, attempting to explain cognitive development, speak of qualitatively different mental operations, abilities, or processes as emerging. Vygotsky (1934) identifies three stages of cognitive development of which the last, concept formation, emerges in adolescence although preliminary forms appear earlier. He writes, "a concept emerges only when the abstracted traits are synthesized anew and the resulting abstract synthesis becomes the main instrument of thought."

Werner (1940) is also interested in the mind's structural properties. According to him, a basic principle of development is a constantly increasing differentiation and centralization or hierarchic integration of function within the developing organism. Werner hypothesizes cognitive development as a sequence of increasing differentiation which, as it moves toward discrete thinking, serves to displace syncretic thinking.[4] Werner writes

> . . . development is creative development. This means that each higher level represents a new entity with respect to the one preceding it, and is understandable in terms of itself. The more primitive level is not to be derived by the subtraction of single qualities from the higher level. Any level, however primitive it may be, represents a relatively closed, self-subsisting totality. Conversely, each higher level is fundamentally an innovation, and can not be gained by merely adding certain characteristics to those determining the

[3] Neural trace theory is not generally acceptable to American psychologists today. However, Gestalt formulations have had considerable influence on many psychologists' conception of the cognitive processes and laid the groundwork for alternative and related theories.

[4] Piaget (1952) discusses syncretism as egocentric thought. He writes that syncretism is the ignorance ". . . of objective relations in favor of subjective relations, to impose arbitrary schemas upon the world of external objects, to be constantly assimilating new experiences to ancient schemas, in a word, to replace adaptation to the external world by assimilation to the self. Syncretism is the expression of this perpetual assimilation of all things to subjective schemas and to schemas that are comprehensive because they are unadaptive (p. 228)." As described by Piaget, syncretism is the thought pattern of the young child.

previous level. . . . In general, the more differentiated and hierarchically organized the mental structure of an organism, the more flexible or plastic its behavior. . . . This means that if an activity is highly hierarchized, the organism, within a considerable range, can vary the activity to comply with the demands of the varying situation.

Hence, as the developing child learns to differentiate he assumes an increasing ability to subordinate and integrate ideas —that is, he develops the ability to think hierarchically. It may then be assumed that the adolescent is well into the hierarchical thinking stage. Werner's point is well taken and particularly appropriate for an understanding of self concepts. When the organism can hierarchize its thinking of self in the sense of subordinating and integrating ideas, it becomes flexible in applying the cognitions it has developed in reference to itself. With higher innovative qualities of thinking or mental activities available to it, the more adaptable and flexible the organism will be to the stimuli demands of itself and of the various environmental situations.

Qualitative Emergences in Cognitive Activity

Elkind (1966) states that by adolescence, thought is not only more logically complex but also more flexible and mobile. A middle-childhood individual tends to stay with his initial strategy, whereas an adolescent, who may start out with a quite complex strategy, is more ready to shift to a simpler one. Children are not as able to distinguish between their own thought products and reality as are adolescents. Although concepts relating to self are constructed from their *own* thought products (egocentric products), self becomes modified by an understanding and awareness of a consensus reality; it becomes the combined result of perpetual self-checking and validation confirmation of concepts by interaction primarily through role behavior with others in the environment.

Wolfe (1963) characterizes a conceptual level as ranging from the concrete to the abstract. At the highest levels the child can adopt the conditional attitude and function at a maximally abstract level with a high developmental power of differentiation. Such persons can infer beyond the perceptually given. Wohlwill (1962), following Witkin's (1962) lead, feels that a decreasing dependence upon information in the immediate stimulus field yields a better conception of cognitive development than does an increase in either powers of abstraction or intervention of symbolic processes. Lunzer (1965) reports that the ability to perform verbal and numerical analogies depends upon the ability to establish second-order relations, an ability that increases with age. Anchoring the process more directly to the environment, Bruner (1966) visualizes cognitive development as "the internalization of technologies from the culture, language, and the more effective technology available."

Kohlberg (1963) notes that younger children are insensitive to individuality and are more authoritarian in their interpersonal relationships than are adolescents. Morris (1958), writing on the adolescent period, states

> Normative expectations become more liberal, responses more flexible and qualified. There is a greater tendency for respondents to be unwilling to give an answer to situations as they stand and to say, "well it depends on a number of different things. For instance, if . . . ," and to specify modifying conditions. Self interested elements also show a change from selfishness to more independent, autonomous responses.

But this differentiation also brings the problem of personal guilt, since the adolescent is able to recognize the reactions of both omission and commission, particularly as evidenced in role conflict. To do what one "should" is often to reject something that one also "should," and so often in real life the "shoulds" are mutually exclusive. This presents a cognitive conflict in need of solution. Both "oughts" relate to expectations held by others as to what constitutes an appropriate role behavior. The implications for self-concepts are obvious.

Value Development in Cognition

Katz and Zigler (1967) see self-image disparity as a function of developmental level which involves two factors tending to increase with maturity: (1) capacity for guilt, and (2) ability for cognitive differentiation. Where self-concept is concerned, the capacity for guilt can be assumed to be determined or created by judging oneself by the standards or criteria composing one's value system. If one "upholds" his values by behaving in accordance with his criteria for them, he describes his efforts as "good" or "ethical" or by some other equally value laden term. If he falls far short of his standards when evaluating himself in accordance with those standards, he may, if he cannot rationalize his own evaluation, judge himself as behaving badly, inappropriately, or unethically. He may redefine his behavior in terms of negative affect feedback due to his behavior styles, or as the incomplete satisfaction of the criteria he has established for attaining the ideals or goals to which he aspires (end states of existence). Thus, guilt may refer to a cognitive-affective response occurring when an individual makes self-reference judgments based on the criteria of his own value system. If the individual's personal value system does not concur with the value criteria used by others for their standard of conduct, the question of guilt does not arise. For example, a sociopath does not feel guilty or diminished in his self-esteem by his modes of conduct. However, an individual value system is not wholly idiosyncratic. It grows out of learning and experience occurring within a given culture, and to that extent is based to a large degree upon society's definition of morality. In the last analysis, morals and morality are simply a given culture's criteria for judging behavior styles or modes of conduct of others. An individual's moral type judgment at any point in time represents a culture based, as well as a personally based, interpretation.

Cognitive Structuring by Cognitive-Affective Motivational Criteria

Where cognitive development is concerned, differentiation occurs when classification has begun. Classification of concepts by organization of "like" or "unlike" elements within specific classes precedes inter-relating these concepts or the manipulation of ideas and possibilities. Cognitive development of classification and ordering establishes the rules, guides, and plans of action by which the organism processes its experiences. Criteria taking the form of rules and standards are characteristic of each developmental level. The development of values may be seen as the process by which an organism sets standards or criteria determining its modes of conduct (behavior) and its end states of existence. An individual's values represent the criteria he has cognitively established for himself out of the manifold of his learning and experience in the cultural context in which he is born. A complication in the application of such criteria, however, is that their processing (encoding) is conditioned by affect.

Social Effects on Cognition

Inhelder and Piaget (1958) note that the transition to formal operations stems from cultural pressures and the adolescent's need to take on adult roles and to exemplify adult modes of thought. As this occurs, the adolescent's conceptual range is extended to the hypothetical and the future. They also note that a maturation of cerebral structure coincides with the type of ability required by formal thinking. Elkind (1966) writes, "What is significant about the growth of the mind in the child is to what degree it depends not upon capacity but upon the unlocking of capacity by techniques that come from exposure to the specialized environment of the child." Piaget (1952) states that at a level of intuitive thought social influences bear heavily on cognitions. Reciprocity and cooperation are necessary prior formations for the development of logical thinking. Braham (1965) points out that peer groups account for the emergence of thinking operations in the adolescent. Social role participation by enabling an individual to assume roles representative of his self-view should increase the progress of cognitive-affective development. Each social situation or role participation offers experiences to the developing individual. Such an individual needs a variety of role assumptions so that he can evaluate as well as define himself in terms of reality.

Hypothetical Bases in Cognitive Functioning

With the emergence of "thinking operations" man becomes an hypothesizing animal. Cognitively, at his highest level he functions by means of hypotheses, and his attitudes, beliefs, and knowledge consist of hypotheses. Even his reaction to himself as a functioning organism consists of a series of hypotheses. But his environment must broaden his horizons so that he has rich sources of material about which to make hypotheses-sources that present a challenge. A wide range of experiences offering him an opportunity to assume a variety of hypothesized roles so that he can see how they work in practice, and so that he can formulate further hypotheses, will offer him optimum conditions for cognitive development. Actually, for effective cognitive development, man needs to be challenged intellectually. To understand one of the most puzzling and exasperating aspects of the adolescent period—their insurgence, unreasonableness, rebellion, contrariness, espousement of peculiar (to adults) causes and activities—one must realize that they have attained a period of life characterized by hypothesized idealism. During this period of idealism adolescents develop hypotheses and thoughts, and postulate ideas by interrelating their criteria in an attempt to achieve their ideals. With additional refinement, modification, deletion, and elaboration of criteria for self-structures, the individual is able to relate his modes of conduct toward achieving his ideals. He develops operationalized *means* (behavior) by which he strives to exemplify his ideals through his behavior. Thus, values determine standards for the means (his behavior styles or modes of conduct) and for ends (ideals or end states of existence). Values are conceptual criteria; rules are behavior-event applications.

Values consist of rules and standards and must be both operationalized and measurable: operationalized in the sense of becoming capable of being achieved through conduct and behavior; measurable in terms of directional attempts at achieving goals or ideals.

The ideals of society should be substantially congruent with the individual's goals. Enforcing nonacceptable ideals on an individual creates a resistance between the individual and his society as he comes to believe that society's values are unacceptable when evaluated against the standards set by his value system. Psychological and behavioral conflict ensue when people are placed in a position where the value based expectations and demands of society are at variance with their self-structures and the underlying value systems they have developed for judging their identities and their behavior styles.

Quest for Congruence of Cognitions and Social Reality

Optimum cognitive development requires that an individual find experiences and roles meaningful to him in his own terms. Such experiences, to be meaningful, must not merely stand surrogate for the past. Rather, they must represent for him projections of an ideal for the future. Erikson (1962) speaks of this aspect of youth as the "capacity for fidelity." He sees it as a strength of youth, although, equally, the quest for fidelity can bring youth and society to a confrontation difficult for both. Erikson's position is that, given the cognitive and interest structure of younger children, fidelity could not develop earlier than adolescence but, "must not, in the crises of youth, fail its time of ascendance." The quest for fidelity can be likened to a sense of trust, confidence, or belief in the ideals one has established, and in the establishment of adequate and socially acceptable criteria as means for achieving such ideals. Adolescent fidelity represents a trust or faithfulness where their beliefs are concerned as well as a developing sense of confidence in the predictability of the environment, particularly as that environment takes the form of society at large. The outcome is a developing sense of mutual confidence about what reality represents.

As youths search for fidelity, they make congruent their hypothesized conceptions with regard to self and reality. As any given adolescent reintegrates and reorganizes his thoughts, he qualifies the concepts he previously postulated. He gains new meanings and new acceptance of self. Although reorganizing cognitions concerning self may create a transitory dissonance, the reintegration of concepts creates flexibility of thoughts, beliefs, and attitudes concerning the self. Such flexibility also creates increased specificity for the meanings and interpretations of self.

Decentricism in Cognitive Functioning

With the ability to decenter a child can evaluate himself from others' points of view, but he again enters a period of egocentric thought at adolescence when he applies his values criteria, evaluates himself, arrives at new self-concepts by hypotheses, and gains new meanings and definitions of himself in the self-constructs he formulates. Only when he submits these concepts to consensual validation can he adopt a reality basis for his concepts of self. In this way he learns to accept a fidelity basis in his quest of truth with respect to himself in society.

Relativity of Temporal Sequences to Self

Perhaps one of the greatest of all developmental changes is that of the individual's perception of time. The very young have no perception of time beyond the immediate even when they are apparently able to manipulate the verbal symbols of time. They live in a world of now and not now which is event-specific. As they progress through middle-childhood they can manipulate and understand the abstractions of space-time, but without reference to themselves as objects, mentally organized as a manipulable symbol of their beings. Eventually, children do develop a concept of time and of causality. There also develops a cognitive permanency to objects, hence, an acceptance of references of self. In adolescence the situation is different because self is considered in formal terms, has become of deep personal concern, and all aspects of the environment have to be considered and hypothesized in terms of self. Time is no exception, but there is still a qualitative difference between the adolescent and the adult in his consideration of time. Developmentally, during adolescence time is seen as a limitless ocean upon which one floats almost in a state of suspension. Time becomes timeless, not necessarily bound by actuality. In contrast, maturity sees time as a rushing stream down which one is propelled with increasing velocity toward a certain end. Time becomes limited by reality and the self-process is considered as finite or as approaching completion of and for the organism.

Chapter 5

Self and Cognitive Theory

JEAN PIAGET, IN HIS FORMULATION of a four-stage sequential theory of cognitive development, has added new dimensions to our understanding of cognitive function and its development over the years of childhood and at least the early years of adolescence. Piaget (1950) writes that intelligence is, "only a generic term to indicate the superior forms of organization of cognitive structurings . . . behavior becomes more 'intelligent' as the pathways between the subject and the objects on which it acts cease to be simple and become progressively more complex." Thus, cognitive development is a dynamic process moving progressively toward greater differentiation and complexity. Its course may be described as a sequential series of levels or stages. Such cognitive functioning and development is the means by which an individual arrives at specific and integrated concepts, self-concept being an example of one such integrated concept although of all an individual's concepts it is the most central and all-pervasive. Hence, the development of self-concept results from the development of cognitive functions. Self may be viewed in the same terms of progressively more complex organizations and structurings between subject and object. The organism interprets itself as both a doer (subject) and receiver (object), or as an actor and a reactor, through its conceptual reorganizations of its transactions with the environment.

Continuing Piaget's analysis of intelligence, he states, ". . . intelligence constitutes the state of equilibrium towards which tend all the successive adaptations of a sensorimotor and cognitive nature, as well as all assimilatory and accommodatory interactions between the organism and the environment." The problem of intellectual growth, particularly as the child passes through the middle years of childhood and enters adolescence, may be viewed as primarily accommodation of prior existing structures. Although assimilation and accommodation are always cyclical in nature as the organism tends toward cognitive equilibrium, the quality of structure development appears to change with increasing cognitive development. Primarily, the young organism is involved in encoding responses which are event specific. With cognitive maturity the emphasis appears to "downplay" the assimilating function but stresses the accommodation of existing structures to new organizations and reintegrations. This cognitive ability is required for hypothesis formulation emerging, as Piaget notes, during adolescence. Assimilation of stimuli appears to be necessary for creating or developing structures whereas, during processes of thinking and reasoning, stimuli presentations are not mandatory for accommodative restructurings of *prior* existing cognitions. However, adaptation requires both processes. Without assimilation stimuli are not brought into the mental schema, and accommodation[1] of structures to new stimuli cannot take place. Previously developed schema become habitually in use or a cognitive "set" results and egocentric thinking occurs.

Cognitive-Self Implications of Piaget's Stage Theory

Piaget postulates four major stages of cognitive growth through which every intact child passes in his progress toward maturity. These stages are the sensorimotor stage, the preoperational thought stage, the concrete operations stage, and the stage of propositional or formal operations.

In Piaget's first stage, the sensorimotor period (ages 0–2), the child begins life with a few inherited reflex-type schema, and as his environment requires it, he develops more complex

---

[1] If accommodation becomes the higher intellectual hurdle, then manifesting the self at any point in time through role taking can be construed as accommodation if it is based on developing internal standards.

motor responses and habits. During this period cognitive functioning is a highly specific event. Actions have yet to be internalized to form representations or thoughts. At this stage the individual's self-reference system is highly simplistic and primarily in the somatic domain with reactions by a largely undifferentiated physical self characterized as satisfaction-dissatisfaction, security-insecurity, or functional control-lack of control. The psychic self requires the power to symbolize with its accompanying ability to organize and discriminate to become operational.

At the beginning of Piaget's second or pre-operational thought stage (ages 2–7), symbolic or thought functions appear. To immediate sensorimotor space is added the complexity of actions remote in space and time. Cognitive classes of objects are developed, although they lack the generality that will characterize a later stage of development. At this point the child begins to develop rules for classifying by identification and by organizing those cognitions primarily through cognitive-affective interpretation of the specific stimulus event. Differentiations begin to lay a groundwork for the emergence of a concept of an ideational although still rudimentary self. Differentiation is the ability to discern uniqueness within conceptually organized classifications. The child is handicapped by the lack of a logical system to which he can fit classes so that he can "operate" on them. This stage may be subdivided into two recognizable substages, the preconceptual and the intuitive. The preconceptual substage (ages 2–4) is the transition period during which the child's previous highly individual event perception is being overlaid with a more general concept of events. Reasoning, insofar as it occurs, is event to event, based on direct analogies but lacking either reversibility or generality. The concepts of self are also transitory. The second substage, that of intuitive thought (ages 4–7), moves the child from intuitive thought, characterized by generality and reversibility. During the second substage, the self-system becomes more flexible and more differentiated and begins to operate increasingly in terms of expectancies not necessarily limited to the events of the immediate environment. The child refers to himself in less time-bound terms. He refers to a past self and can discuss it in relation to the present situation.

During the third or concrete operations stages (ages 7–11), the child develops operations implicitly based on the logic of classes and relations, although the operations lack the combinational possibilities characteristic of the succeeding stage of formal operations. During this period, the child's operations are concrete in that they are concerned with reality, exemplified by real objects that can be manipulated and "subjected to real action." The self at this point can be cognitively interpreted as an object apart from its subjective orientation. It is both I and me. The self, when treated as an object, becomes interpretable and meaningful as a third person object in the cognitive structure and capable of assessment of performance effectiveness. During this stage, the child can begin performing roles according to societal and self-expectation of appropriateness. The child's personal performance becomes important in specifying and exhibiting identities. The developing self now begins to test reality, although there are limitations. At this time in the developmental sequence objects not present can be replaced by more or less vivid representations which stand for reality. The child cannot yet deal in the verbal domain with simple hypotheses involving *reasoning;* he has to rely upon the prelogical intuition of the early stage if forced into a situation demanding hypothetico-deductive reasoning.

During Piaget's fourth stage of cognitive development, that of propositional or formal operations (ages 11–12 to 14–15), the child no longer confines himself to perceived data from his immediate temporal and spatial environment. He can deal with information across the barriers of space and time in probabilistic terms and is free, if he wishes, to reconstruct reality. His thinking becomes propositional and he can interrelate propositions. In order to achieve this status of formal thought construction, the adolescent must be able to apply operations to objects by mentally performing various actions on them, and he must be able to "reflect" these operations on pure propositions which have replaced objects. Piaget (1967) writes that, "concrete thinking is the representation of a possible action, and formal thinking is the representation of a representation of possible action," and in this sense is "thought raised to the second power." Thus, formal operations are applied to hypotheses or propositions, while concrete operations are applied to tangible objects. This is their crucial difference. The child who has entered Piaget's fourth stage is able to draw conclusions from pure hypothesis without having to rely on actual observation. It is during the stage of formal operations that the individual is able to form hypotheses about himself as a separate though interpersonally related functioning entity. He is now able to attribute to himself qualities which he can attempt to implement through the various roles he adopts. Thus, the organism hypothesizes itself and builds expectations and behavior which test its hypotheses against reality. Characteristically, the proposition-capable individual posits a self which he expresses operationally by various definitions of "I." He speaks of himself in terms of "I am" and "I am not." The "I" now stands for the hypothesizing self together with all of its pronoun elaborations which cognitively define and interpret the organism to itself and others.

Central to an understanding of the fourth stage is the adolescent as a hypothesizing, system-building organism. Contrasting the thought processes of adolescents and pre-adolescents Piaget (1967) observes, "By comparison . . . an adolescent is an individual who constructs systems and theories." This can be expanded to include a self-system and a theory of its application. Certainly the child, bound as he is to concrete thinking, does not build theoretical systems, nor does he abstract theory-based common principles from data. He deals with each problem in isolation. Insofar as children have "theories," they are informal ideas and thoughts and are largely unformulated in any coherent fashion. His "theories" proceed from actual reality based experiences integrated to provide him with a series of postulates. In contrast, the adolescent with his facility for elaborating abstract theories, is constantly engaged in hypotheses and theory formulation frequently unrelated to everyday realities. They are not constricted by *present* time or event orientation. His theories can be or are hypothetical deductions proceeding from hypotheses of probabilities of occurrences. How do adolescents handle their theoretical formulations? Equipped with the ability to think formally, the adolescent can reflect and theorize spontaneously and characteristically will be found to play with his newfound power as he finds before him new worlds which he tries to incorporate into himself by a process of egocentric assimilation.

Egocentric Assimilation

Piaget (1967) writes, "Adolescent egocentricity is manifested by belief in the omnipotence of reflection—it is the metaphysical age *par excellence;* the self is strong enough to construct the universe and big enough to incorporate it." During this period, the adolescent is aware of but is not bound by reality and may occupy in his imagination a world construed without reference to the actualities of everyday life. Gradually, as the individual moves through adolescence, he increasingly is able to gain control of his formal thinking capacity and put it to work rather than to treat it as a unique new toy. At this point in cognitive development the individual posits many interpretations of himself and tests the feasibility of his assumptions through some form of social participation. His ability to reflect upon his prior experiences enables him to predict and anticipate in terms of self-expectations. In fantasy he can be anything he can imagine. In reality he learns that some things he believes about himself have a greater probability of occurrence than do others. Formal thought and reality become reconciled and, as Piaget points out, the adolescent comes to perceive that the proper function of reflection is to predict and interpret experience, not merely to contradict. This represents attainment of a new equilibrium which leaves behind the metaphysical egocentricity of early adolescence. Thus, it appears that the egocentric and narcissistic stance occurs in immature individuals whenever the system receives input which causes them to appraise, analyze, and cope with ideas not previously in their thinking. An adolescent first learning about social action, political action, or other similar matters tends to become quite egocentric and narcissistic in his approach.

Egocentricity is conditioned by the situation in which it occurs and the subject matter upon which it operates. The same individual can show egocentricism in some matters and not in others, depending upon when each input occurs and the extent to which it represents a new cognitive field of action. Performances typically measured by the Piaget experiments usually appear earlier than do the more social action oriented matters of later adolescence. All we can say is that, as maturity is approached and achieved, the areas of egocen-

tricism decrease although, prior to maturity, any newly introduced area will tend to elicit egocentric behavior, whether in
the area of sexual behavior, political action, or "higher aspects
of ratiocination." Piaget (1967) notes that "every transition
from one stage to another is likely to provoke temporary os-
cillation" with the result of "provisional disequilibrium."[2] Individual differences and specific special situations aside, as
adolescence proceeds egocentricity is displaced by greater degrees of selflessness, but the advance is uneven, as Gardner
(1962) notes of development in general.

Self-Cognitions as a Development Sequence

Cognition is a process whereby an organism becomes aware
or obtains knowledge and meaning of an object or of events.
In developmental psychology cognition is primarily considered concept formation, problem solving, and the thought
processes. Any individual builds a conceptual system, through
which he views not only his world but himself as well. Developmentally, the issue deals with the level of cognitive manipulation available to the individual as he builds his self system.
As the individual grows older he moves toward greater abstract behavior as he passes through various levels of cognitive behavior.

The foregoing discussion indicates that in the course of its
development the self-process may pass through consecutive
levels: (1) egocentricism (selfishness); (2) sociocentricism
(self-other mutuality); (3) extra-self integration (self-society
reciprocation); and (4) self-transcendence (selflessness). In
the first level, egocentricism, the individual relates selective
responses to the environment. The result is primary integration and organization, classification, and development of rules
of action with affective feedback of the individual's responses
to the environment. The second stage, sociocentricism, is characterized by the individual's ability to understand others as
he learns to relate his own rules to those possessed by others.
At this level, role taking results from self-decentering condi-

---

[2] Piaget made this statement with reference to movement from stage
to stage in his four developmental periods, but it applies equally well
to movement within a stage.

tioned by the affect which modifies the individual's cognitive structures in social interaction. The individual modifies and elaborates his self-cognitions as a result of his social transactions. He learns to structure his behavior according to others' expectations and can accommodate the demands of the situational context. During the third stage, extra-self integration, the individual assumes a higher level of self-evaluation as he bases his behavior on his own modified values, identity constellation, and conscience. His actions are not based solely on others' judgments nor on personal anxiety and fear of failure, but instead find their source within the internal structure of his own assemblage of hypothesized and substantiated identity concepts and his modified value system and are in closer relationship to reality. During this stage, the individual's modes of conduct (behavior styles) are related to personally determined end states of existence taking the form of personal ideals or conscience.

Self-transcendence is the highest level of self-development attainable. It evolves from the possession of a flexible and secure value system broadened and specialized for self-evaluation so that the individual is able to transcend his personal boundaried ideals and aspirations in keeping with a universal value criterion for judging self and mankind. The self becomes interpreted as broader ideals rather than as individual conscience.[3] Such ideals are based upon benefits to mankind rather than upon personal rewards or individual gains. The level of development appears to sublimate the self in preference for a universal codification, but in reality man becomes maximally rewarded because he has defined himself in terms of all men and women and thus becomes limitless. His sense of self-autonomy, originally created by placing the locus of control within the self, is not only responsible to itself, but is enhanced by the extension of self to others. The self-concept now encompasses fellow man and is maximally enhanced. The boundaries of self become unrestricted.

The foregoing discussion of cognitive development places

[3] By no longer being "a stranger" to himself the individual does not become estranged from his fellow men. He seeks a unity with his ancestors and contemporaries so that by planning for the future of his progeny he is able to perpetuate his ideals by transcending his present limits of mortality.

within the individual the formation of a system that perceives and interprets actions and processes information. The system operates on the basis of concepts and hypotheses, formulating rules of reference resulting from learning and previous experiences. Concepts of self are very personal concepts. They develop cognitively and affectively from the experiences of the organism with its surrounding environments.

Attitude and Value Aspects of Self

A self-concept is a concept developed by cognitive organization and the dynamic process of development. It constitutes a series of beliefs and attitudes about the organism. Attitudes are organized beliefs focused on specific objects or situations predisposing some preferential response. Attitudes are the result of cognitive organization of concepts with attached affect. Self-concept, because it is a concept, is cognitively structured; because it consists of attitudes and beliefs it is affective. Hence, self-concept may be defined as a value-based cognitive-affective symbolization of the organism growing over time through maturation and the accretion of experience. Perception of self is a percept based on values because values are considered to be criteria for modes of conduct or behavior and end states of existence. A person develops rules in his cognitive processing. Such rules are the organization of decisions specifically applied. Values are criteria and standards for determining and for assessing the application. If an individual develops attitudes and beliefs about objects during concept formation, he also develops attitudes and beliefs about himself as an object. Such percepts as, "Johnny is a good boy, a bad boy, a sad boy, or a tall boy" have been cognitively processed with traces of affect arising from interaction with the environmental agents that helped structure the concept. It may be assumed that if an individual develops attitudes and beliefs about objects and situations and determines the behavioral response he judges as appropriate, then that same individual also develops a system of attitudes and beliefs that judge his own modes of behavior with himself as an object. Such judgments are part of the value system of that individual and are part of his self-reference. Early in life comments about a child, or his behavior, become a label or a sign (a preconcept) of a hypothesized identity (a cognitive interpretation giving meaning to the self). Prior to the ability to formulate concepts, before categorization and classification are cognitively accomplished, these labels or signs repeated occasionally with an attached affect by others, become part of the individual's cognitive-affective organization and as much a part of his self-references as were the repetition of his gender and name. Such signs are combined with others to form the individual's self-hypotheses. Self-concept formation consists not only of information gathered from the processing of experiences but also of the beginnings of criteria for the evaluation of what is good or bad, preferred or rejected. When used by the young child in describing himself, the awareness of these self-identifications also include the emotions and sensations they were associated with, and these, in turn, become conditioners of total cognitive structure. For example, a boy not only relates his cognitively correct gender but also may refer to himself as a "good" boy. Others' evaluations are processed into his cognitive structures enhancing and modifying the individual's attitudes and evaluations of his conceptualizations of self and form the basis of the primary hypothesized identities.

Throughout ontogenesis, various dynamic processes emerge and develop as an individual follows the normal progressive development of his species. One of these dynamic processes is cognitive development. With cognitive organization, an individual becomes capable of hypothesizing about the self through discrimination, integration, differentiation, and interpretation of concepts he has formulated. The concepts are ideas of reference, images, beliefs, and attitudes the individual has cognitively organized, defined, redefined, and evaluated through application of and association with reality.

Identity Formation

In order to understand the process of identity formation, one must first accept the premise that identities, at least to some extent, grow out of various identifications, but that identity and identification are not interchangeable nor identical concepts. Identification is the cognitive affective process of selective organization of perceptions which become preferential to

one individual in a given transaction. Identity is the individuation of perceived, unified ideas or elements differentiating an
individual from his identifications. Identities are conceptualizations of self that develop out of combinations or fragmen-
tations of identifications. Perceived and hypothesized ideas
are manifested with reference to the self in social interactions. Many of these ideas of self are hypothecated in role
relationships, and are operationalized and testable in reality
based performances. Thus, while identifications are prerequisite to the process of self-development, the concepts relating
to the developing self are manifested through the positing of
identities helping to define the cognitive-affective interpretation of the self in its various stages of development.

Chapter 6

Meaning and Identities

WHEN SPEAKING OF AN INDIVIDUAL'S CONCEPTS OF SELF and their underlying formative processes what is really at issue are the meanings he attributes to himself both as a person and as a participant in situations involving other persons. Meaning is essentially a problem of the cognitive process of relationship and patterning.[1] It may be construed as an integrative principle enabling an individual to interpret his past, present, and future in self-relational terms. Meaning finds its motivational base in the fundamental drives for synthesis and completion as well as in the needs and values representing extensions and elaborations of those drives. An individual's behavior is essentially determined by the meanings he has constructed.

In the preceding chapters on cognition it was indicated that one of the outcomes of the processes of cognitive development is the individual's acquiring a universe of interrelated meanings comprising his reference system for the assessment

[1] Osgood *et al.* (1957) note that meaning is a cognitive state identified with ". . . a representational mediation process." They speak of meaning as involving ". . . that process or state in the behavior of a sign-using organism which is assumed to be a necessary consequence of the reception of sign-stimuli and a necessary antecedent for the production of sign responses. Thus, for Osgood meaning is a relational or process concept, a position with which the present writers concur. Boring (1933) argues that meaning is always in context, while Lewin (1951) writes that, " 'meanings' depend on embeddedness and—multiplicity of embeddedness makes for multiple meanings on various levels of discourse."

of all incoming stimuli. A meaning originates when a stimulus event is cognitively processed and located with reference to previously acquired meanings. Thus, the stimulus event's locus in the experiential universe of the individual determines the event's meaning.[2]

The experiential universe consists of an unlimited number of interrelated meaning loci and may be characterized as multi-dimensional space (temporal, spatial, and directional) without boundaries or fixed form. The lack of boundaries refers to the amount and extent of organization of encodings (assimilation) into the experiential universe, but does not negate the limits imposed by maturational and genetic factors presented by the unique individual as well as by the genetic limits of his species.

The cognitive act of processing and locating a stimulus event in the experiential universe of meanings represents assessment behavior. During assessment behavior an individual, using his reference loci, endeavors to find a relationship locus for a new event or for the relocation or confirmation of a previously encountered event. Relocation involving change and revision of the original relationship location of an event represents reassessment behavior. No meaning locus need be static. The individual's experiential universe may be in a state of flux.[3]

Relative absence of reassessment behavior represents a deprived environment, limited mental capacity, rigidity or increasing selectivity. Developmentally the tendency is to move

---

[2] The writers are not positing either an isomorphic theory of brain function nor a spatially identifiable map of meaning locations within the brain. Explicitly, no attempt is being made to correlate the physiological processes of the brain and conscious psychic experience. The system here proposed deals solely with inferences about psychic experience and process and hence represents a hypothetico-deductive theory of an aspect of cognitive behavior. The fact of a relationship between mind and brain and of the probability of existence of neural correlates of conscious experience are not denied, but we agree with Sherrington's (1933) statement, . . . "the relation of mind to brain is still not merely unsolved, but still devoid of a basis for its very beginning."

[3] No event, once attended to and located can ever be forgotten. It is always present and potentially usable whether the individual is aware of it or not. Attention to a related event or locus may bring it into focus.

toward decreasing reassessment behavior as well as toward increasing complexity in the sheer number of events attended to, processed, and located. Reassessment behavior declines after the second decade of life as increasing selectivity filters out attending to events that would have been attended to earlier in the developmental sequence.

That an experience is cognitively processed does not mean that the experience is reflected or incorporated into the experiential universe as an exact image of the environment. The experienced event, derived as it is from perceptions and actions on the part of an active-reactive individual, can only be brought into the system if it can be made to *fit* by its relatedness to other processed experienced events.

"Learning" assumes that the organism is establishing a pattern in its experiential universe by establishing a relationship of experienced events enabling a locus of reference to be created for the present stimulus. As a dot can be located in a spatial plane so can it also be related and located in as many planes as can be made to include that dot in their geometry. In a similar way, each experienced event is brought into the system because it can be located by reference to previous events and can thus acquire meaning. For a new meaning to be formed the event (as in the case of the spatial dot) has to be related to other meanings previously acquired. As was previously indicated, such relating may cause reinterpretation of previously established meanings by readjustment, elimination, or rearrangement of the events included in the meaning field.

When an event has been processed and has taken on meaning, and when the circumstances of the individual call for action further types of behavior including analytic and implementation behavior may follow. Analytic behavior occurs when behavior (action) is called for but the loci do not clearly indicate what is to be done, but a decision has to be made. Reassessment behavior is usually present when analytic behavior is required. Implementation behavior occurs during a period in which an individual is using in his internal and external behavior the reference loci he has and is, in effect, manifesting them in his behavior. A further type of specialization is synthesis behavior representing the Rogerian concept of playing with elements and concepts. Synthesis behavior is an initial step in a creative production.

When a number of loci are taken together, each locus having acquired a meaning due to its location in the experiential universe, they form an integrated unit to represent a concept. Such a concept is a meaning field consisting of an aggregation of meanings, a dynamic "pulling together" of loci into a consciously attended field. However, such a field is not a unity in one location in the experiential universe into which pertinent events have been assembled. It represents a patterning of attention upon a "whole" set of appropriate events wherever located. The example of the spatial dot indicates that a meaning locus can exist in as many planes as are included in the experiential universe.[4] Thus, a meaning field is a flexible arrangement or patterning of relationships and a basis for formation of a concept. A human organism is capable of forming a multiplicity of concepts. Of these, concepts of self are most central in directing and governing behavior and are necessary for an individual's recognition and application of himself as a personal entity.

Any concept of self held by an individual represents an aggregation of self-reference meanings existing as a cognitive-affective structure. Such self-reference meanings are self-interpretive and self-evaluative. Components of this self-reference aggregation of meanings together with components from other concepts of self held simultaneously by the individual are selected to fit various situations as they arise. At any point in time these selected, interpreted aspects form an assembly of self-reference meanings making an identity. Thus, an identity is a self-assumption of the situationally selected self-reference meanings of the organism occurring at any point in time. An identity is how an individual defines himself when confronted by a given context and is called into being only when circumstances demand a self-reaction.[5] In this sense an identity is a self-hypothesis.

---

[4] Such a dynamic patterning of loci is an intra-field organization of concept formation. In contrast, a grouping of loci not included in that particular meaning field is an extra-field aggregation.

[5] The relation of values to concepts of self is discussed in Chapter 7. A system of values becomes incorporated into the self-meaning system of the individual and is called into being when an action decision has to be made. In this way values are operational in the formation and behavioral exemplification of any given identity.

A person's self-hypotheses and the further cognitive action states to which they lead consist of a large number of different concepts of self as well as a potentially unlimited number of situation-related identities. One of an individual's developmental tasks, if his development is to follow a normally adjustive course, is to arrive at some integration of both his concepts of self and his identities and to display in his behavioral application of them some self-consistency. This could lead to an over-all self view, heavily dependent upon the evolved value system, that transcends specific self-concepts or identities and is generalized across situations.

In behavior an identity is implemented by the taking of a role. A role taken is a concrete behavioral manifestation and implementation of one or more of an individual's identities, presenting to the observer a picture of the identity in action.[6]

The identities discussed to this point are self-hypothesized identities representing an individual's picture of himself for a given situation or purpose. This is not to say that an individual may not possess an *aspiration identity,* which is either what he is striving to become or what he wishes he could become even though he has no hope of attaining it. This may be a combination of role taking in behavioral manifestations and role figmenting through covert behaviors.

But man is a social creature interacting with others who perceive his behavior, make judgments about him, and, in effect, define him by attributing to him an overall self-generalization or frame of reference. The realities of the environment and of an individual's capacities also enable, demand, or require him either to take or to play various roles, and through these roles to perform in accordance with an hypothesized identity or cluster of identities, or as others expect him to behave. Is a hypothesized identity the one others perceive or is it the one the realities of the environment permit to operate?

[6] Roles may be performed which are non-representational of an individual's identities but meet his perceptions or expectations of social and cultural demands. This is role playing. A role having no relation to reality but representing an individual's fantasies may also be assumed. Such role figmentation may but does not necessarily represent any of an individual's conceptualized identities. Thus, roles may be taken, played, or figmented. A definition and discussion of role behavior appears in Chapter 9.

The answer is neither, for an individual's self-perception may be in accord neither with the perceptions others have of him nor with the roles the realities of economic and social life force him to play. An individual's behavior not in accord with an hypothesized identity is an anti-identity. An anti-identity is manifested in role playing behavior. The manifestation of identities or anti-identities will be perceived as qualitatively different to both observer and role assumer. The coping behavior involved in dealing with these types of identities is the focal problem in the development of a stable, flexible self-structure, particularly during the second decade of life.

In the case of an identity perceived by others any individual has numerous perceived identities, probably as many as there are perceivers. Different people interpret the same person differently, depending on their relative roles and the situations in which interaction takes place. Yet an individual's pattern of behavior can be such that there is considerable commonality in the views most persons have of him.

The writers differentiate between self-concept and identity and do not use them interchangeably. An identity is a result of a dynamic cognitive process of selecting meaning components of various self-concepts to form an assembly of self-meanings. In this manner identities emerge from combinations of self-concepts. The self-process produces an identity hypothesis with the result that the individual is able to verbalize to himself and to others who and what he is. Thus, an identity is a self-construct evolving from the physical-physiological development of a living organism possessing awareness, hence mind. Such a construct must of course be based upon a series of decisions which have to face the test of reality in role behavior.

A separation of self-concept and identity poses a situation in which an organism is postulated as perceiving itself through its own self-concepts and expressing the perception as a series of identity hypotheses to be tested in the form of role behavior. This reasoning obliges us to assume a self-process, but it does not lead to the further assumption that the self-process is infallible since one of its products, identities, are only hypotheses growing out of self-concepts held and, like all hypotheses, may prove to be untenable when tested against reality. However, when an hypothesized identity is confirmed by reality the identity is more secure and a further step has been taken toward ultimate individual maturity of self-acceptance and self-knowledge.

Since identity is defined as a hypothesis made by the organism about itself, it is important to examine the individual's intellectual ability to hypothesize. Here the formulations of Inhelder and Piaget (1958), discussed in Chapter 5, have relevance since they enable us to understand what approaches an individual uses at the various developmental stages as he builds his hypothesized identities.

During the preoperational period a child begins to be aware that objects may possess more than one dimension. He then begins to establish invariances. During this period his play, fantasy, and imagination develop symbolic schemas. Role taking and role playing also begin. Until the child can conceptualize that a person can be many things at different times, he himself, cannot role take. Role taking can occur only when the child is able to perceive and attribute certain styles or patterns of behavior to others. Before he can actually reality test a role he must be able to decenter.

At first a child's concept of a role is not definitive. He cannot accept the idea that a daddy and an astronaut are one person; one is either always a daddy or always an astronaut. The child has a preconcept of a daddy. He does not clearly understand that persons or objects within class memberships can be different from one another or that they have a commonality in their class inclusion. With time and experience, a child begins to perceive the requirements of each role individually and realizes that a person can be different things at different times. Thus, a daddy can be an astronaut and not cease to be a daddy. This is part of establishing the rule of invariances and conservations.

When a child acquires a word that labels a class of objects or actions, he has the beginnings of a concept based upon class inclusions and class exclusions. He can relate data from his past experiences and arrive at judgments. There also develops some stability and permanence in the concepts.

The child's perception of each role as having separate behavioral attributes provides the foundations for role assumptions either in reality,[7] play, fantasy, or imagination and is

---

[7] The development of perceptions of reality is conditional with cognitive development levels. A child tests what he thinks exists. As his cognitive-affective structures gain finer elaborations, through con-

part of a developmental process. Play is not frivolous; it is important to the developing child and can become a rehearsal or preliminary for many roles that may be available to him in the future. Prior to a child's ability to role take his gender identity must have some permanence. Otherwise the child does not engage in hypothesizing an identity for role taking but resorts to imitative type play, a form of social learning of behavior attributes and expectations.

Piaget reports that during the chronological age period from 7 to 11 the child exists in a concrete, simplistic world. His approach is descriptive and he limits himself to the raw data of his perceptions. He classifies, orders data in series, and sets up correspondence. He does not isolate the factors involved or embark upon systematic experimentation. He is able to tell who and what he is, but he does not speculate or ask what or why he is. He accepts himself without question on the basis of the data at hand.

According to Piaget, the child begins a final period of operational development (propositional or formal elements) at about 11 to 12 and reaches a peak at 14 to 15. During this period he develops the ability to reason by hypothesis—that is, he can now accept any sort of data as hypothetical and can reason from it. Thought no longer proceeds from the actual to the theoretical, it starts from theory so as to establish or verify relationships between things. Instead of merely coordinating facts about the actual world, hypothetico-deductive reasoning draws out the implications of possibilities. Thus the adolescent tries to discover all possible combinations in order to select the true and discard the false. He typically begins to form hypotheses about himself which he then feels impelled to test against reality. When the hypotheses so tested are found inaccurate they must be modified or dropped. A child who hypothesizes a brick wall as made of glass and tries to see through it encounters reality, just as when he hypothesizes the

---

sensual validation or verifications and perceptual self checking (Murphy & Spohn, 1968), his interpretation of what he perceives as reality undergoes refinement. This refinement occurs as a result of experiences which modify previous cognitions. He includes the results of his interactions with others as affective feedback modifying his cognitive constructions.

bricks as made of air and walks into them. One means of ignoring reality is to "make believe" and play a game "as if" one can really see through the bricks. Children often do this and we call it imagination. When adolescents do it we are less understanding and call it daydreaming or fantasy. But in either case, the matter becomes serious when, refusing to accept reality, the individual clings to his original hypothesis that the bricks are made of air and continues to act as though they were indeed air. In its more massive forms, we call this psychosis, and in its less massive, neurosis.

Gollin (1958) maintains that hypothesizing about the behavioral or personality attributes of others is a cognitive developmental process. Initially the child can solve problems with conflicting information by using unitary type concepts. He perceives all the information pertaining to one dimension and disregards all else. Later in development he builds concepts in parallel. He classifies all attributes into each proper dimension but treats each as a separate, functionally independent idea and he does not attempt to interrelate them. Eventually the child reaches a level of cognitive development where he can integrate conflicting and multi-dimensional or multi-conceptual information as an interrelated composite. He can integrate, hypothesize, and test as well as organize and classify. Thus, reality testing of role taking behavior is a part of the developmental process and dependent upon cognition of role attributes and an understanding of reality.

The matter is not simple, for with the integration of experience hypotheses become integrated-related and whole constellations of hypotheses must be depended upon as the individual builds his personal meaning of self. During the process of building self-concepts each individual develops a hierarchy of identities consisting of those identities and clusters of identities that have been tested either by actual performance or through fantasy or play. An identity assemblage or hierarchy is a complex organization consisting of identities that are tested by taking roles. Role taking consists of perceiving certain styles or patterns of behavior attributed to others as important or necessary to the situation. The types of roles that are taken during different periods of development are influenced by one's needs and values.

To test one hypothesis against reality is, in effect, to test a number, and to find one inaccurate or insufficient and in need of modification leads to the need to modify a number of others. Obviously, some tests of reality are indeed crucial and may lead to some exceedingly major changes in the identity hierarchy. When resistance is encountered the changes may have far reaching effects on the individual.

Actually the individual is in search of himself. Previously he accepted what he found and did not question it, nor did he have any particular reason to defend it. During his self development he hypothesizes, rejects, and feels the need to explain, relate, and interrelate his identities for self-interpretation, definition, and meaning.

However, although the individual is capable of trying to discover all possible combinations and to discard the false and select the true, he must still operate under certain limitations. Affect, habit, and the stereotypes engendered by previous experience exist.

One of the dilemmas of the self-process is that the more important certain identities are to the identity hierarchy, the greater risk incurred in role testing, especially in the case of those identities associated with peers, family, and occupations. If role taking attempts are unsuccessful a person is likely to experience stronger affects from these unsuccessful attempts than from other threats to the identity clusters.

The individual may attempt to alleviate some of the negative affect to the identity structuring by rearranging the complex of the identity hierarchy by assigning higher importance to other successful identities. But rearrangement of the identity hierarchy does not always occur free of complications and the result often is floundering, cognitive dissonance, and the manifestation of defense mechanisms. Defensive behavior may force the individual to operate at an earlier stage of his intellectual development. Everyday life does not always operate in a logical ordered world of mathematics and physics. The individual often perceives and uses incorrect or inaccurate data provided by his culture and his previous experience.

Thus, a hypothesized identity can be exemplified in behavior by the individual through his performance in roles as role taking behavior. The resulting role performance leads to enhancement, modification, or change in the identity hierarchy. To the extent that a person is able to perceive accurately the pertinent role attributes and to abstract and integrate the relevant aspects of a given role, the perception may be viewed as a cognitive-developmental process dependent upon the stage or level of cognitive functioning attained.

Exteriorization of an Identity

As an individual's identity hierarchy is evolving from his self-concepts, or even after an identity is well formulated, tested successfully against reality, and integrated into behavior, the individual may exteriorize his identities—"give them away," so to speak—to some person or object in the actual or hypothesized environment. An individual may depart so far from reality that he is able to build for himself, and even surround himself by, a false or imaginary environment incapable of being sensed by others. The individual's degree of belief in and the completeness of his acceptance of this hypothesized environment is an index of his contact with reality. Some individuals become so immersed in their imaginary environments that nothing outside is real; they may be said to have retreated from the world in order to live in a figment of their own imagination.

In the cartoon series *Peanuts*, Linus carries an old blanket about with him and refuses to be separated from it. For Linus, the blanket becomes himself and in effect stands surrogate for him. The blanket is Linus. To separate him from the blanket is to separate him from himself; nothing is left when the blanket is gone.[8]

For most of us the idea of projecting our personal qualities onto inanimate objects is quite bizarre. A human target for such projection seems more appropriate, although, psychologically, the two are equivalent. It may be necessary to con-

[8] This becomes a concept formation of homogenous perceptions from which elements or aspects within this classification are not cognized as unique or different. This concept formation is not exactly synonymous with primary identification but is the reintegration of self to non-self leading to unity. There is no longer a differentiation of a hypothesized identity, as individuating self from others. In exteriorization the individual projects (transfers) his self-hypotheses to others whom he perceives as self rather than non-self entities. In this way he denies the reality of the others but creates them as he hypothesizes them to be.

sider the somatic and the psychic identities separately when investigating exteriorization, for it is probably impossible to give away somatic identities, except in cases of the kinds of hallucinations people experience through lack of adequate stimulation or through boredom (repetitive redundant stimulation) where "detachment" or exteriorization of the somatic from the psychic (ideational) self occurs, or in cases of sensory deprivation, drug or alcohol ingestation, or cognitive drift.

Integration of Identities

Late in the second decade of life, as the moratorium of middle adolescence draws to an end, the normally developing individual is faced with the task of self-definition. To achieve his goal he must clarify and articulate his hierarchy of identities and integrate them into an evolving system of values. The roles he takes to implement himself are judged by others against a harsher, less flexible reality than usually characterizes childhood. Facing emancipation and the commitments of maturity the neophyte adult has to make and apply assumptions about who and what he is in many cases before he feels secure in his self-definition and its supporting tests of reality. Unanswered questions and lack of experience complicate the process.

In his theory of psychosocial development, Erikson (1950) represents adolescence as a time of seeking final integrated identities in the face of complicating environmental and personal factors which promote role confusion. This, according to Erikson, leads to a crisis in which the adolescent tries to evolve a new sense of self from his previous identities and values, a self which must lead to meaningful goals and behavior compatible with those of the peer group. Erikson, supported by studies such as those by Bronson (1959), Howard (1960), and Howard and Kubis (1964), concludes that the core conflict of adolescence is identity formation versus identity diffusion. According to Erikson, the other conflicts of adolescence may be subsumed under the main conflict and include: self-certainty versus identity consciousness; time perspective versus time diffusion; anticipation of achievement against paralysis; and sexual identity versus bisexual diffusion.

A characteristic of the later years of adolescence, and on into the early years of maturity, is the increasing primacy of values over needs as instigators of behavior. In the earlier years of development physiological and the associated, elaborated, or socialized needs have primacy and from them stem values. But in middle adolescence needs begin to stem from values[9] as values serve to create behavioral directions and behavioral styles in keeping with the individual's evolving concepts of self and in conformity to universally accepted gender concepts.

An adolescent successfully resolving the identity crisis will regroup his childhood self-conceptions into new patterns resulting in a rearrangement of an identity hierarchy. If he gains a greater degree of social support for a particular identity the relative importance of that identity in his hierarchy will increase. Each interaction (role taking) involves a test by the individual of a hypothesized identity or set of identities. The role response may give him positive, negative, or no social reinforcement or acceptance and will drastically affect the need-gratification that resulted from the role enactment.

Identities are not of equal importance to the individual. Those having greater importance within his value system are those that result in greater personal conflict if they do not gain social support from significant others. During adolescence social roles relating to major developmental tasks are tested, hence the result is a period of maximal rearrangement of the identity hierarchy for all phases of his life including peer and family relationships and occupational aspirations and choices.

Eventually the adolescent defines himself and sets up a hierarchy of expectations in which he has confidence. His interpersonal relationships become harmonious and reciprocal; he will be secure in his self-perception, and he will have confidence that others' perceptions of him are relatively congruent with his own. He evolves a secure inner identity hier-

[9] The ultimate primacy of the life-sustaining physiological tensions of the organism cannot be denied. Given conditions of stress, need for biological homeostasis, and functional organism perpetuation, the physiological tensions do assume at least momentary primacy. Such resumption of primacy may, however, in some individuals lead to resistance and conflict.

archy and feels that he is an accepted member of society.

The individual who has not been successful in his resolution of the conflict and whose "identities are diffuse" will present the alternate picture. Bronson (1959) reports four interrelated specific characteristics of the identity-diffuse person: (1) lack of continuity between past and present; (2) high degree of anxiety; (3) less certainty about present dominant characteristics of self; and (4) fluctuations in feelings about self. The identity-diffuse adolescent lacks inner referents (standards and criteria for self-evaluation) to which to anchor new experiences; he lacks adaptability and fluctuates between unbending resistance and overeasy compliance. Essentially the identity-diffuse person is dependent, often to the point of passivity, despite his occasional resistances.

Lomas (1965) notes that passivity represents an abnegation of natural authentic development. It arises in an environment which discourages action and rewards parasitism. The passive person often accepts an identity assigned to him or copies an idealized identity. He does not reality test through role taking of hypothesized identities which are congruent with his value system but role plays, performing a role in keeping with the demands of others, though not necessarily based upon his perception of the requirements of the role nor of his self-needs. Thus, role playing can lead to role confusion. Adults encourage such acceptance in their young as they lay down the rules of a "good" and a "bad" person. In Victorian times women were the victims of such passivity. The current adolescent unrest and alienated behavior may well have as its basis role assignment by elders which, if accepted, could lead to identity confusion. Identities can be idealized and idiosyncratic as well as conventional conceptions of self-representations. We reality test these identities either individually or in clusters, overtly through social role taking or covertly through imagination, play, and fantasy. The reality of life is the testing ground for the feasibility and relevance of a hypothesized identity to the social situation. Havighurst (1946) posits one of the developmental tasks that leads to social approval and, if successful, to happiness as "the acquisition of a set of values and an ethical system as a guide to behavior." Using this as one of the tasks facing adolescents, each role a youth takes must be related to his value system and therefore becomes a basis for self-reference and self-evaluation. Each role that is promoted and projected upon him by significant adults, as culturally and socially sanctioned, must be acceptable to his critical self-evaluation and net him the rewards and satisfactions that are necessary for his developing self-exemplary behaviors. Many roles must be explored in our imagination, daydreams, and pretense play prior to actual performance in real life. Some figmented or fantasied identities are discarded and never overtly role tested while others through the "try-out" phase are practiced in anticipation of the time when they may actually be tested (e.g., a college student imagining himself a teacher, or a girl playing mother). Even though some roles never materialize they reinforce identities if successfully and satisfactorily performed, covertly as well as overtly, and hence reinforce the individual's identity hierarchy. The adolescent who has difficulty developing a self-concept to the point of being identity-diffuse[10] uses the "different" or outgroup person as a target for the attribution of his own self-doubts as his means of finding closer identification with the peer group and of setting up a personal defense.

In general, a person who lacks role participation gains little experience and does not enhance his cognitive-affective structures. Because of his limited cognitive experiences, the individual does not develop adequate or sufficient criteria to judge or evaluate self and others. He must resort to developing or accepting stereotypic roles and often may seem intolerant and idealistic.

[10] True to some extent of all adolescents at some period in their progression through adolescence, and of any individual at transition points in his adjustment to changing conditions, both self and social.

Chapter 7

Values and Self-Process

VALUES PLAY AN ESSENTIAL PART in self-process. An individual's development of values goes hand in hand with his development of self-concepts, making consideration of the problem of self impossible without including values as a functional aspect. Early in life, values resulting from the process of socialization are incorporated into an individual's self-reference system and find manifestation in the attitudes he expresses, either overtly or covertly. A value or set of values assumes a guidance function when an action decision must be made. Operationally, a value is a meaning representing the conceptualization and elaboration of a rule.

Processing Input Data

Self-as-process depends on both awareness and experience. Experiential data entering the individual's cognitive system by means of the afferent mechanisms of the perceptual modes utilized are encoded and processed as inputs. New inputs are related to the individual's previous inputs to comprise his reference field and derive meaning from their relative location in that field. Such location represents a cognitive evaluation of the input and requires use of a storage and recall system or memory index, as well as the ability to integrate and differentiate experiences.

The psychological activity permitting the processing of input data and the related generation of output information has been compared to the mechanical operations of computer systems. The analogy, however, is not tenable since computer performance inadequately represents the dynamics of human cognitive performance. Computers do provide comparative match-mismatch analysis, but affective and evaluative processes resulting from qualitative comparisons are not possible in computer performance.

Computer models are both seriational and comparative systems employing progressive or cyclical analysis by accretion or quantification of input experiences. The human organism is also a seriational, comparative accumulator of experiences, but its experiential universe which is correlational and interpretable in qualitative degrees is not always dependent upon increasing the interactive experience levels of the human organism for generating information products. The ability to generate qualitative decodings of inputs provides the organism with discriminating and evaluating processes or functions enabling the derivation of interpretations or meanings from its environmental experiences. In short, the human organism has the ability to store its perceptual data by contextual evaluation.

Reference Loci and Standards

Ontogenetically, the development of an evaluation process proceeds from the earliest or primary interactions of the organism with its surrounding world and its own physical entity. Stimuli arising from its own somatic-physiological processes and stimuli presented by the surrounding contexts, when attended to, are brought into the cognitive field of the individual and interpreted only if comparisons by reference loci can be established. The establishment of reference loci is a qualitative-comparative process permitting evaluation of the present stimulus event and interpretation of the stimulus cues to be made so that meaning can be derived from any given experience in terms of the organism's experiential history. This process is not a *maximization* of discrepant experiences, but a comparative analysis process of *optimization* of intensity and discrepancy of deviation of what has previously been experienced as well as what is currently being attended to. The ability to discriminate, interpret, and provide meaning to stimuli is a cognitive-affective function. When criteria are formulated and ascribed to objects, events, and behavior during an individual's cognitive development, these standards are called values. Values are the system ascribing or systematizing criteria and standards for behavior and for directionality of behavior.

Values and Cognitive Processes

Results of activity by and upon an active organism also involve reactive conditions. Such behavioral configurations are the genesis of awareness and evaluation, for when stimuli are repeatedly presented, discrimination and affect become part of the behavioral sequence. Since a developing organism can react to repeated stimuli with patterned behavioral responses it may be posited that, from these stimuli responses, rudimentary cognitive structures (anlagen) are constructed from sensory-affect and discrimination, providing the genesis of a value criterion. When inputs or experiential encodings are optimally, although not necessarily maximally, variant to the cognitive system and when aspects of the stimulus-event experiences are redundant to the historical universe of the individual, then abstractions or differentiations of meanings can be constructed of the present event with self as central to the organism's interpretation of its interaction with the contextual stimuli.

Early in the developmental sequence behavior is an event-specific experience. Responsiveness is a total organismic effort. With repetition of stimuli affective criteria or linkages are established, each as a specific datum, and condition cognitive structures. Patterns of responses are provided for the pleasure of reproduction, as intrinsic to the behavior, by self-initiation of activity. Experiences and the affect modification of the cognitive processing of these encodings become complex constellations of reference loci. To insure that the processes of discrimination and evaluation cope with the complexity of the experiential universe, symbols or a coding system must develop and be employed. Symbolization, or codification, is possible through emergence of a denotative system such as language. A value continues to be a discriminating element when connotative variations are added to the original denotative symbols. Such variations reduce information to a personal, coded form permitting the individual to conceptualize his experiences in terms which provide him with self-references and personal meaning. This does not presume that self-references representing instances of conceptual development of self-as-process can only be evaluated through the use of a structured language. Somatic perceptions are self-percepts based upon sensory-motor awareness of the body as a bio-physical entity. Perceptions are sensory-motor-affect inputs to cognitive structures and, as such, are modifiers of cognitions. Perceptual inputs are also dependent upon awareness, permitting an evaluative estimate to be made of the experienced stimulus event. Language, or the development of a coded system of symbolization, provides a representational surrogate for specific perceptual events and objects by providing codification and synthesis to data for cognitive-affective assemblage and assessment. With variations of perceptions and conceptualizations, an enhancement of value criteria ensues. Discrimination of experiences and affective processing of behavioral feedback additionally refine evaluative standards as pleasurable or noxious, good or bad. Values emerge from discriminative, comparative bases in the form of perceptual-conceptual systems of criteria or standards resulting in modes (conduct) and directionality (goals or desired states) of behavior.[1]

While sensory motor functions originally provide the frame of reference from which self-perceptions emerge and are evaluated, motor activity becomes disjunctive in its applied importance to value development. Overt manifestations of behavior are, or can become, replaced by symbolic manipulations of conceptualizations of self, thus extending the spatial-temporal directional perceptions of self beyond its physical boundaries.

The assumption explicit in the foregoing discussion is that values represent a system of evaluative criteria formulated by the individual during his process of development. Values develop from the inculcation of cognitive-affective encodings of

---

[1] Many writers have discussed the development of values and the relation of values to attitude formation. Among these Rokeach (1960, 1968), Rosenberg (1965) Kluckhohn and Strodtbeck (1961), Smith (1949), Scott (1959, 1965), and Woodruff and Di Vesta (1948) are most relevant to the present discussion.

the results of learning, imitation, and reinforcements and are reached inductively from behavior. Furthermore, values also are acquired through longitudinally developed socialization efforts either directly or vicariously with significant other persons.

Values and Selective Responsiveness

The human organism is a composite of functional systems. Its structures and their concomitant functionings cyclically reincorporate to develop it into an active-responsive system characterized by responses, directional behavior, and low grade stimulus hunger. The organism encodes and discriminates new environmental experiences by means of their affective-perceptual influence upon his cognitive system. These interactions eventually help the human organism to perceive itself as a physical entity in its environment and to evaluate its functional effectiveness in its environmental interactions.

The primary tasks of the organism are to help locate, articulate, and control components of its own physical entity and to develop responses and coordinations leading to self-control and environmental manipulation which is designed to satisfy selected stimulus hungers. Shoben (1962) refers to these tasks as the "selective responsiveness of the self-process." Behavior is action oriented over the entire course of an individual's life, but of particular importance are the affective and discriminative processing of the results of specific action-event sequences by the infant as he learns to react to his caretakers as facilitators of his needs and as providers of his experiences. Such social interactions enhance the development of value criteria by providing variable experiences for derivative data of the infant's somatic self-perceptions. Social caretakers, primarily the parent or parent surrogate, interfere with the satisfaction of those biophysiological needs inherent in the infant's physical living state. These tissue preservation needs possess a consummatory function which is met by effecting an elaboration within the cognitive-affective system from the processing of reinforcements and rewards. The reinforcements are affective feedback emanating from the infant's somatic demands upon external figures (the non-selves) and from his competence and effectiveness at meeting his own demands. Such cognitive-affective processings provide lower level values based upon discrimination of effects of the infant's behavior, establishing worth, goodness, badness, and pleasure standards by the results of his actions. Thus, somatic percepts, emanating from a biophysical base, developmentally emerge as basic criteria for determining behavior and as standards for the person to evaluate his own actions.

Needs and Values in Self-Process

Psychological needs are learned extensions and elaborations of fundamental drives and physiological tension states, operative in determining the direction and intensity of an individual's behavioral action or line of action, and thus a force in his cognitive processes.[2] They develop goal-directionality as the result of experience and socialization. Functionally, an individual's psychological needs are operative in self-processes, the development of his needs being an aspect of his development of self-concepts. Hence, we may use the terms psychological needs and self-needs interchangeably.

In a real sense, need-induced behavior is a manifestation of the self and may take the form of either self-indulgence or self-exemplification. Self-indulgence needs focus primarily upon the satisfaction of physical appetites and their socialized elaborations. They are, of course, highly egocentric and to a large degree hedonic in character.[3] In contrast, the self-

[2] The presence of a need, whether or not the organism is actually aware of it, indicates a lack or deficiency in the organism and ordinarily leads to the organism's activation. A goal is an end state or result whose attainment reduces or leads to the cessation of the need-induced activation. Between the need and the goal lies behavior. English and English (1958) write, "Most psychologists hypothesize a personal or an organic determiner of the behavior that is not wholly a function of the need. For this need-instigated, goal-oriented determiner motivation or motive are the most general terms." They note, however, that it is possible to speak of need without postulating an intervening variable, in which case need becomes a substitute construct for motive.

[3] Some writers speak of self-indulgence needs as physiological needs. It is the position of the present writers that all needs have physiological origins and are elaborated and given direction by experience and socialization, one group of needs transcending physical appetite satisfaction (self-exemplary), the other remaining throughout an individual's life quite specifically in this area (self-indulgence).

exemplary needs focus upon a more idealized exemplification and perpetuation of an individual's concepts of self. But, whatever their later developmental direction, both self-exemplary and self-indulgence needs are derived from socialization and elaboration from the primary value criteria of somatic origin. These early value criteria set satisfaction or a consummatory state of somatic needs as the primary goal. Self-needs are instrumental in achieving directionality by changing and modifying individual behavior. When values are applied as rules for event specific behavior, the goals become the objectification of the needs that the value criteria have created by ascription of standards to certain behavioral styles or modes of conduct. During the formal stage of mental operations, following the advent of puberty when hypothetical and propositional thinking occur, the value system gains primacy.[4]

Thus, developmentally, in the early years of an individual's life needs of a more self-indulgent nature have primacy, but as value-based propositional thinking begins to occur, values dictate the behavioral direction with correspondingly greater emphasis upon self-exemplary needs as self-representative. With this shift in emphasis needs, then, are formed or elaborated by values serving to mold and define identity concepts of self into a stable, flexible conceptualization. Those identities or concepts of highest significance in the self-process are most representative of values held tending to take precedence in an individual's actions.[5]

---

[4] In the years before adolescence, needs arise primarily through learning; whereas, later when needs are formed primarily by values and secondarily by learning, the learning aspect is deemphasized in favor of a more affect laden approach.

[5] The transition from a focus upon self-indulgence needs to a focus on self-exemplary needs provides possibilities for internal self-conflict. Throughout an individual's life there is a certain amount of fluctuation as the two areas of need-striving, often mutually exclusive, endeavor to gain ascendency. In this zone of conflict a basis for neurosis or psychosis is often found, although it may also be a breeding ground for the more adjustive mental mechanisms. Eventually, the ravages of age on the physical structure cause the value system to yield to the self-indulgent needs. Senescence brings the individual full circle to an emphasis upon end states characteristic of his early years.

Evaluative Standards

As an individual interrelates his conceptualizations of self and evaluates himself in terms of their effective manifestation, his value criteria are the standards he employs for self-evaluation. The choice of roles he takes to exemplify an identity concept represents goals (objectives of his self-needs) or behavioral modes directed by his value system. During the developmental sequence, concepts of self are assessed by two processes. The more ideal concepts of self representing the individual's inner view of "this is what I actually am" are based upon and formulated by the criteria established by the more idealized aspects of the value system. Such concepts form a frame of reference that often has to be modified or even abandoned in actual role behavior. The operational concepts of self, actual self-manifestations, are also evaluated by use of value criteria but they are based on perceptions of reality demands and find manifestation in role behaviors. These two processes for assessing concepts of self provide discrepancy data for determining self-attitudes, self-esteem, and self-satisfaction.

As a person develops over the course of his life span, he evolves a system of evaluative criteria which become increasingly modified and discriminatory toward preferential standards of comparison and judgment. With increasing experience, the evaluative criteria become qualitatively more discriminatory of past experiences.

Rules are the organization of decisions specifically applied. Values are criteria and standards for determining the application and assessment of the outcomes of rule application. Thus, while rules provide the organization with event-specific action decisions, the evaluation, interpretation, and meaning of the behavior, the event and the objective (goal) of the act can only be determined by the criteria ascribed by the values held by an individual.

Values can be inculcated, as Martin (1954) and others have indicated, through the learning of behavior by imitation and reinforcement, the cognitive encodings of these actions, and by definition reached inductively from behavior. Values are also acquired through social interaction processes over a period of years, first from the parent or parent substitute, and later from other persons with whom the individual associates either directly or vicariously. Reading and the communications media generally are also a significant source of value formation. Values give direction to the end states of existence (goals of life, as self-fulfillment) and set standards of behavior and social conduct. In this manner they represent the individual in the self-system through his identities concepts. All of an individual's specific identities are representative of his value system to an extent that a substantial equation exists between the identity concept constellation and the value system. Probability of selecting an identity for a given situation, as in role taking behavior or even its inclusion in the identity concepts constellation, is normally a matter of the exemplification of the values held.

Thus, a person's values ascribe the criteria for application of the rules for his conduct and represent standards by which he evaluates his participation in various roles for the testing of a hypothesized identity. While values are cognitively structured they are always conditioned by the affectivity resulting from prior actions, experiences, and beliefs.

Values appear relative, for throughout development they are constantly modified, elaborated, or refined as a result of, (1) past experiences, (2) cognitive restructuring of information and actions, and (3) environmental circumstances. The roles a person takes and the behavioral directions he manifests are determined by these three conditions.

Attitudes and Ideals

Values are often expressed to the outside world by the enunciation in word or deed of an attitude indicating preferential reaction to or feeling about a person, a thing, or a situation. Such attitudes are the manifested aspects of a directed (focused) value in the cognitive-affective system.

Attitudes are important to the value system and to the self-process because they are based upon certain organized beliefs. Beliefs, in turn, are based upon cognitions structured in the cognitive-affective system. By this interrelationship, attitudes are inherent in the value system, although on a lower level of organization. Attitudes are habituated behavioral responses (overt and covert) specifically focused. Values for the self-process are the criteria developed from discrimination of sensory-motor actions forming bases for rules and are further elaborated as criteria and standards of conduct (modes of behavior) and end states or goals of self. As compared with attitudes, values are more fundamental, dynamic, and pervasive.

In the popular literature, one often encounters the term "ideals," the assumption being that an "idealistic" person is somehow a person apart, a person of a rarer kind; visionary, perhaps, but commendable as long as his involvement in the practical affairs of reality is kept to a minimum. In this approach, ideals are often interpreted as of a different, and perhaps superior, order than values. In actuality, an ideal is simply an expressed directive or objective of a value, or the ascription of evaluational criteria to a specific end or goal. Ideals may be aspirational and usually represent a desired end state. Hence, an attitude relates to an ideal in the same way it does to a value—it is an expression of a preferential way of reacting or responding to events permitting one to take a role that will lead to behavior needed to achieve the ideal or ascribed value. For example, to achieve the ideal world (or a world predicated upon one's value criteria), attitudes to sanction activities directed toward that end would be needed, and they would have to be considered right and acceptable.

In behavioral terms a value is a conceptual standard ascribed to an act, object, event, or end state, while an ideal is a product or end formulated as exemplification of a directional outcome or result; it is, however, still possible to agree with conventional usage to the extent that some values may be categorized as involving outcomes extending beyond the purely hedonic criteria of the individual. The self-system of some individuals furthermore contains a larger than usual proportion of "altruistic" values, and such persons can indeed be called "idealistic." Adolescents, for example, due to inexperience and inadequate testing of reality, are often quite idealistic because they have yet to visualize the world as it is or, perhaps, to accept human nature as determined by a considered consensus of opinion. Mature idealists who, despite adverse tests of reality, maintain their idealistic self-stance are usually non-conformers in social role demands unless, of course, their idealistic expressions of personally held values solely take the form of role playing[6] in social interactions and never of role taking of concepts of self.

The "idealistic" person then is one who emphasizes ideals over reality. A person who is idealistic about human social relations accepts the constructs of altruism and self-abnegation as standards of behavior. That is, his values are expressed as ideals and determine his behavioral styles or modes of conduct. A person of high ideals will think of himself as honest, loyal, and interested in the common good. What is more, he will expect the same attitudes and behavior of others. Often the idealistic person will discount reality and expect people to "rise above themselves" and to have "good" motives. The idealistic person must make severe adjustments when confronted by reality. The validity of one's ideals also needs consideration. No one could possibly question the desirability of possessing certain ideals, but as a human being, one must live with others; standards that are so high, so unreasonable, or so capricious that they are impossible to fulfill are not amenable to reality testing through role taking and, hence, are unfortunate for both the individual holding and aspiring to achieve them and for those obliged to associate with him.

A characterization of the idealistic person or of the person who possesses "high" ideals implies that his ideals are such that society accepts and recognizes them as good. That is to say, the idealistic person possesses value standards that have been enhanced, reinforced, modified, elaborated, and ascribed to as desired ends or states of purposive existence resulting from reality based experiences. On the other hand, an idealistic person can be subverted in his development of ascribed standards for social conduct or modes of conduct. For him, behavior antithetical to socially approved or moral behavior may represent perfection, or an ideal state, yet in his way and according to his values, he may be an exceedingly idealistic person.

Bizarre behavior and ideals are not necessarily the result of disturbances in the development of perceptual-conceptual processes. Such behavior results from the interpretations

---

[6] See Chapter 8 for a discussion of differences between role playing and role taking.

derived from past experiences and the discrimination and differentiation of value criteria from the cognitive-affective processing of the experiential universe of the individual. Thus his value criteria and ideals are idiosyncratic to his interpretations and meanings of self.

Values are relational, interpretive, evaluational schema processed from an individual's past experiences and are part of the cognitive-affective information system serving to formulate his rules for decision making. For example, the juvenile delinquent may conceptualize his ideal self as a criminal and may exemplify in his behavior and attitudes great loyalty toward criminal ways and persons. Society would hesitate to think of such a person as an idealist, yet in his own subverted way, he is.

Values as Self-Expressive

The discussion of values and self, to this point, has taken the position that a value in the individual's self-process can exert strong pressure for expression through identity conceptualizations exemplified in role taking behaviors. This assumes that values are a systematized organization in a relative structuring. Individual differences are evidence that some individuals become more flexible in applying their value standards than are others. Persons more flexible in their value criteria application of self-concepts in role behavior are less apt to assume role playing behaviors representative of identities they feel are not really their own. For such persons environmental demands requiring anti-identity behaviors and responses will simply be rejected even at considerable affective and cognitive dissonant expense. The problem of conformity in self-behavior is particularly difficult for persons whose concepts of self have yet to achieve stability in self-conceptualization.

Some persons have a value system allowing them to express superficial or synthetic attitudes serving to conceal real feelings and values. They *play* certain roles or assume false or elicited identities with little difficulty. Society expects social conformity from its members, providing proscriptions and sanctions when deviation from prescribed behaviors occur. Many individuals conform, at least superficially, because they feel they must to avoid conflict with proscriptive demands. It can be an exceedingly lonely business to reject demands and expectations upheld by popular opinion. The matter of role conformity is especially important in adolescence since the adolescent peer group tends to be less tolerant of deviation than are other groups.

Social Aspects of Values

A person learns, as part of his social adaptability, that his values should be applied in both a discriminating and a flexible manner. At the same time, he has to be able to recognize that some values may not realistically be applied in every situation he encounters. In the final analysis, only the individual can apply his value criteria. He alone must face others' reactions to his application unless, of course, he involves others with him in his activities to the extent that they must share in the reactions and evaluations such application calls forth. Particularly difficult for an individual is to deny the desirability of the values his peers hold. Insofar as these values conflict with those of significant persons such as parents, teachers, or employers, the individual may face adjustment difficulties; acceptance and approval by one side means rejection and disapproval by the other.

Conformity to social role demands frequently is a source of confusion. The groups to which an individual belongs are often inconsistent in their acceptance or rejection of his various attitudes and his exemplifications of self-concepts through role behaviors. Honesty may be highly lauded in school and in church, but dishonesty may elicit the greatest admiration from the juvenile gang, the world of work, and sometimes from the home or various subcultural groups. Loyalty to a significant figure or to a representative of constituted authority may involve disloyalty to other significant figures. Courage may have a purely physical interpretation for some and a moral one for others. Since situations are interpreted and meaning applied to them in terms of a value criterion, the interpretation of events, contextual situations and social interactions is idiosyncratic to the cognitive-affective processes of each individual. His manifestation of concepts of self is dependent upon his interpretation of the role opportunity in terms of his self-demands.

Interferences in Expression of Values

For the developing person two main sources thwart or block the manifestation of hypothesized identity concepts. The first results from cognitive immaturity and lack of social participative experiences, leaving the person unable to cope adequately or effectively with his environment. The other is conflicting role demands involving the application of value standards to desired but conflicting goals. The latter problem may take either of two directions. Often in life an individual is confronted with a desired object so closely associated with a disliked object that attainment of the desired object means attainment of the undesired object as well. The second direction conflicting ascribed values may take presents the individual with two highly desired but mutually exclusive goals. This introduces a new element, since both goals are acceptable; the conflict lies in deciding which to accept. If the goals possess equal importance, the individual is indeed hard put to make a selection or, having made it, to be entirely satisfied with it. Fortunately, other associated elements are taken into consideration and the choice is made easier by the dissonance that ensues. However, there is no assurance that a choice once made will be permanent, or that the individual may not regret his choice. As a matter of fact, a goal attained often seems less desirable than a previously competing goal which, at the time of competition, seemed to have a decidedly lesser valence. Or the individual may find that the goal object does not fulfill self-demands. In such a case, there will be dissatisfaction with the goal and a consequent lessening of the motivational force which impels behavior designed to reattain or to keep the goal object. Some goal-directed behavior, particularly among children learning to cope with their environment, is purely exploratory and serves an information-seeking purpose. At times an attained goal becomes less challenging than an unattained one, particularly in the exploratory phases of development. On the other hand, an attained goal object may be so reinforcing that the individual is strongly motivated to keep attaining it, particularly when the goal object represents a high valence need. In this case, a circular action is instituted in which the satisfactions derived from the goal object causes even greater motivation. The value criteria are ascribed to the act itself and not to the end or outcome of the action.

Values and Experiences

In general, values and their accompanying attitudinal expressions develop from interactions with the possessor's environment and the experiences to which he has selectively attended. But the effects of an environment are pervasive to the extent that, with increasing age, people in the same environmental contexts tend to develop attitudes conforming to those persons in their environment who share similar roles.

People need experience in the process of decision making to enable them to make valid decisions concerning their self-concepts. Much of this experience can be gained through social interactions in which the individual reacts to others' evaluations of his postulated identities. With increasing social evaluation, he refines his own developing standards and, in doing so, begins to discriminate criteria for evaluating self by relying less on externally conditioned standards. With approaching maturity, through the application of values, the individual relates self to the development of individual conscience. An individual requires social participation in the form of role opportunities to test the adequacy and relevancy of his judgment and self-standards. He also needs an awareness of his limitations and requires social support to implement his decisions. Sanford (1967) notes that the development of full social responsibility requires experience in social action or in actions helpful to other people. As Sanford sees it, a person needs this participative experience to test the adequacy of his judgments and to familiarize himself with the limits of what he can do. And, of course, he needs support in carrying out the decisions reached if they are to be maintained. Newcomb (1963) notes that a recently changed attitude is likely to persist if one of its behavioral expressions is the selection of a social environment which supports the changed attitudes. Thus, through social role experiences development of social and self-responsibility can occur and can be related to the assumption and adoption of social roles and the exemplification and substantiation of self-concepts.

Chapter 8

Concepts of Others

Development of Concepts of Others

As the individual develops his self-concepts and adapts himself to the environment of objects, he must also develop concepts of others as social objects. The earliest perceptual and conceptual formations are those central to self. From these the child learns to construct his world, and himself as part of his world, by perceiving his own behavior and reactions. Since a child is also a product of bio-social influences (Sherif, 1962) his interactions with other people result in his learning to restructure both his conceptions of self and of the social environment in terms of expectations of predictable effects.

The conditions leading to development of predictable or stabilized expectations emanate from an individual's perception of his own organism as an entity, the articulation of his functional component parts and the differentiation of others as interactive non-self entities. Continuous differentiation of his body and its behavioral effects upon the surrounding social objects and the effects of the surrounding environmental objects upon him requires constant and increasingly complex interactions and the assessment of different experiences. Through the interactive influence of socialization (originally through primary social agents such as parents or parent surrogates) combined with a symbolic code for communication consistency in concepts of others is developed. Other people become necessary for the full development of the individual as a psycho-social human organism.

As a child's interactions become wider and more varied in reference scope, his conceptualizations of self are enhanced, modified, and altered, resulting in his postulating new identities for experimentation and exemplification in role taking behavior. However, unless fairly stabilized concepts of others are formulated, there is no consistency in the behavioral exchange. A lack of constancy of generalized concepts prevents an individual's understanding and interpreting others as structuring his social environment through roles or social positions. This development of concepts of others is part of a social learning process in which he is a cognitive-affective-evaluative participant.

As a child develops cognitions from experience with others, he is able to perceive certain behaviors, attitudes, and reactions as homogeneous with his expectations. Such primary homogeneous perceptions are integrated and assessed as identifications of self with another person perceived as inclusive of a class of self reference attributes. Eventually concepts are reorganized as discrete aspects of behavior, attitudes, and self percepts. They become specific self references further differentiating self from other.

Through interactive feedback of both word and deed others exert an influence on a child's cognitive constructions. Young children behave consistently in social transactions, according to constricted rules and expectations for each other's behavior (Piaget, 1932). Flavell (1963) concurs that social role taking and social participations encourage the development of reciprocity with others and a mutual acceptance. Reciprocity and mutuality eventually result in modification of roles which govern expectations of social acts.

With significant others an individual imitates, models and performs behaviors he perceives to represent others. This behavioral phenomenon is conducive to learning roles in the social environment. Through his modeling and imitation a child gains evaluative feedback about his performance by the qualities of acceptance or rejection of his behavior by others.

A child's cognitive ability to conceptualize others as both similar to and different from his own concepts of self is functionally facilitative for *mitsein* or co-existence with others. By co-existing with others he restructures his self-concepts and exemplifies them through role behaviors by interacting with others in social roles. The results of social interactions help him to make finer discriminations between self and others, to acquire self-meaning as a unique individual, and to locate and define himself as a member of his social group.

As a child develops his self-concepts and fits them to the environment he must also develop concepts of others. By a process of *exterior figure socialization* he assigns roles to various significant *surrogate representative* persons in his environment and lets each of these stand for a category of persons. Such role assignments develop working concepts the child employs in testing of hypothesized identities in reality contexts. But a child can only take a role after he has some cognitive basis for defining a role, such as what a mother does, what a teacher does, what a good boy does not do.

Exterior figure socialization may be a positive idealization of the surrogate representative or it may cast him in an adverse and punitive role. Some of these figures may be those the person has actually had contact with, but others are known only vicariously through reading or hearsay, or through imagination. The delinquent who has had a bad experience with a specific police officer uses him as a surrogate for all police officers; or the school dropout sees an "unsympathetic" teacher who gave him trouble as the prototype of all teachers. Conversely, the youth who has had a good experience with a given police officer or teacher may see these classes of persons from the vantage point of the two "good" ones he knows. Another person, idealizing a politician whose biography he has read or whom he has heard described in favorable terms, may view all politicians in this light.

Reflexive Nature of Others to Self-Process

Reflexiveness is the act of reflecting or directing an action back upon the actor. Reflexiveness, as a psychological dimension, involves the individual (the doer or actor) and other(s) in interactive behavior. By its nature, it is a feedback principle by means of which the effects of a person's actions are assessed as cognitive-affective data. These data may be either self-concept modifying or performance related.[1] Self-reflexiveness is the feedback of others' evaluation of an individual's role taking behavior encoded and processed as modifying, enhancing, altering, or substantiating his hypothesized identity manifested in role behaviors.

Obviously the individual's concepts of self bear a direct relationship to the concepts others hold of him. He uses others as part of the reality testing of an hypothesized identity. Naturally he is most favorably inclined toward those persons who confirm his own self-conceptions, and he is eager that those he likes or admires see him in a favorable light. As Wurster (1961) notes, we want to be esteemed most by those we esteem most highly; when significant others' conceptions are unfavorable, we tend to reanalyze our existing self-concepts even though such reanalysis may be painful and, in some cases, vigorously resisted. The process of evaluation becomes reflexive; one becomes able to evaluate, and act toward one's own person in the same manner one acts toward others, and by the ways others act toward him.

Significant Others

Significant figures play a confirming role in self-definition. Macher *et al.* (1962) report, "The evaluation expressed by others brings about related changes in the individual's concepts of self. It was found that the approving and disapproving reactions of certain 'significant' others were followed by corresponding increases and decreases in subjects' evaluation of self." We all need the reinforcement of others as a confirmation or as a basis for reassessment of our concepts of ourselves. Suinn and Geiger (1965) point out that self-acceptance and acceptance of others are positively correlated, and Backman *et al.* (1963) note that the greater the number of other significant persons who attribute to a person traits that he himself feels he possesses, the more resistant he is to change his identity hierarchy. On the other hand, when one feels he possesses a trait significant others do not seem to

---

[1] Chapter 10 contains a discussion of the difference between reflexiveness as a condition relating to self-concepts and to performance criteria.

perceive, there is a tendency, as Backman *et al.* (1963) have reported, to relinquish the trait with less struggle. The key here is whether or not the perceiving person is significant to his self-evaluation.

The person who assumes that a single person is a representative of a whole class initially overlooks individual differences existing within a class of persons. Inevitably the person will encounter class members who do not conform to his stereotype for that class. He then must cognitively come to terms with the discrepancy and, in effect, change his system of values. Thus, other people have an influence on the value system of any given individual. A change in one's values is cognitive-affective reorganization due to reassessment and reinterpretation of others' reactions toward him. His values become increasingly more affected with decentrism, resulting in and from reciprocity and mutuality towards others. As an individual's values change and ascend in importance as criteria for modes of conduct and end status, his criteria for ascribing evaluational data become more definitive and discriminating. These criteria are continuously reassessed as they are ascribed to role surrogates and to hypothesized identities exemplified in roles.

An individual eventually operates under a system in which his values have ascended to a primary level for evaluating his complex of identities. Where reality-testing involves too great a discrepancy between supposition and actuality of role behavior expectations, the individual may display problem behavior responses and may change his surrogate representative from favorable to adverse. This usually involves a struggle and the individual frequently blames himself for what he perceives as a change in a class of persons. This attack upon his self-esteem is partially based upon the degree of successful achievement of those goals which reflect his values.

On the other hand, problems also arise when the person with an adverse role view finds his cognitions inappropriate or inaccurate when a favorable representative of a class is encountered. In particular, delinquency rehabilitation centers and schools for problem youths must cope with the difficult reorganization involved in the reassessment and reevaluation of a role representative concept or with the defensive behaviors of the individual who refuses to alter his adverse surrogate concept even after disconfirmation. Cognitive as well as affective change results, although resistance to change usually occurs during cognitive assessment of the discrepancies.

Relationships to Others

Considering an individual's relation to others we cannot fail to note the influence they exert upon him and what he perceives himself to be. Yoshikawa (1960) writes, "The adolescent's self-consciousness has as substance much that relates to the feelings and attitudes towards other people. . . . (They) are two or three times more conscious of negative criticism than of positive criticism." Yoshikawa notes that an adolescent's greatest joy, sorrow, suffering, or anger are frequently aroused by the approval or disapproval of others, conditioned to a large extent by the security of the identity hierarchy. As Walster (1965) notes, a person whose self-esteem is temporarily low tends to like another person who is affectionate and accepting more than does a person whose self-esteem is momentarily high. Zimbardo and Formica (1963) report a study in which fearful persons affiliated with others significantly more than did those who were not fearful. For their subjects, the correlation between self-esteem and affiliation was negative. Except in the case of withdrawal, relatively strong self-perceptions and fairly stable, flexible identity structure are necessary for an individual to remain intact and unmodified without reinforcement from others.

Homans (1958) discusses human behavior in terms of exchange theory, proposing that a role becomes an interaction process rather than a social position. The amount of extrinsic reward offered by role-taking in relation to intrinsic need gratification is what is valued by the participants in an interaction. Role-taking includes perceptions, expectations, and styles of behavior in the response patterns. Role taking, therefore, can be related to the quantity and quality of self-involvement expended in terms of the accruable need benefits in each situation. If beneficial, then that identity related to the role taking behavior gains higher salience in the hierarchy structuring than if the rewards (perceived and processed as substantiating his role behavior by significant others) are not granted. This is a reflexive process of evaluation. The available, demanded social roles that are likely to gain an individual the greater benefits are more likely to be enacted if they are congruent with his values.

Self and Reference Groups

Individuals become differentially selective not only to stimuli present in their physical world, but also to stimulus objects, in the form of other persons, in their social environments. An individual cognitively defines similarities and differences between specific others and groups of others, reacting preferentially toward them. Due to his developed cognitive operations an individual is not limited to cognitively-affectively relating himself to others immediately present. He can relate and make references to others either in his situational context, or to others spatially and temporally absent.[2] Thus, an individual's reference groups may be varied in both time and place, overlapping or conflicting in attitude preferences and views. They may even be hypothetically constructed as part of his self-perceptions. In this manner an individual can simultaneously feel a part of many reference groups depending on his self needs and the situational context in which he finds or places himself.

The peer group plays a large part in an individual's conceptualization of identities because there he can test out his self hypotheses while he relates to others. Peer relationships are, therefore, particularly important in the formation and maintenance of an identity hierarchy leading to stable yet flexible self meaning. Manis (1955), using a six week interval, reports an increase in agreement over time between an individual's concepts of self and his friends' perceptions of him. Kipnis (1961) notes that adolescents' self-concepts over a period of time become more like those of their best friends. In a sociometric study consisting of two testing periods, six weeks apart, Kipnis reports that subjects who evaluated

---

[2] This type of reference group relatedness occurs on a hypothetical conceptual basis. The reference others are not perceived in the immediate reality contexts, but are postulated as possible hypothetical relationships.

their best friends less positively in one testing, in six weeks tended not only to change their best friends but to decrease in self-esteem, while those who evaluated their best friends more positively both maintained the relationship and increased in self-esteem. Zazzo (1960) reports that most adolescents see their peers as more socially at ease, more stable, and more generally relaxed than they see themselves. However, he feels that such a conception of others serves as an incentive for self-development, and noted that the discordance between an individual's conception of himself and that of his peers is a necessary stage in development. Goslin (1962) seems to agree with Zazzo when he reports that adolescents rejected by their peer groups tended to overestimate themselves and to show more self-conflict. Goslin also reports that adolescents who perceived themselves differently from the way they were perceived by others in their peer group or were unable to predict how the other members of the group perceived them tended to be isolated from the group.

When all is said and done, building self-concepts and a self-meaning is a lonely task even though the context in which it is often tested is a social one. As one builds concepts of self for self-meaning he must, as it were, face himself. This can only be accomplished alone, and therefore a need for solitude (Lindbergh, 1955) to analyze, re-analyze, and consolidate is very important. Pressures, unfortunately, militate against opportunities for solitude, particularly in a culture where social interaction and the "group" are held to be so important.

Chapter 9

Role Interactions of Self and Others

Function and Nature of Role

An individual organizes his world by structuring roles and their behavioral expectations from cognitive-affective-evaluative processing of behaviors attributed to significant surrogate representatives in his environment. Roles and their representational figures structure an individual's social world by providing him with concept categories derived from specific behavior-event interactions. Roles are functional concepts useful for reality testing of self-hypotheses as well as for adapting an individual to the social demands placed upon him.

Roles provide a means for social participation. Through social learning effects and by socialization techniques of the significant others in his world, an individual learns to expect and anticipate behaviors characteristic of certain role figures. He cognitively-affectively processes direct and vicarious experiences acquired through actual interactions, imitations, modeling, hearsay, imagination, and reading. In this manner he derives expectations and meaning for the roles he encounters in his social movement. Roles provide a means to exemplify identities for consensual validation by significant others in compatible or interactive social positions. These functions indicate that roles are social structures of positions and allocated statuses consisting of a knowledge of behaviors expected and demanded by the social order.

Role Performance

Role enactments consist of those behaviors perceived by an individual as appropriate to situational demands imposed upon him. Equally, they may consist of behaviors imposed upon the situation by the individual's self-system regardless of the situational expectations of others. Such self-demands represent behavioral outcomes directed by an individual's impulsion to achieve certain desired end states or goals.

A role may be overtly or covertly performed and may represent any of several possibilities of an individual's concepts of self. For example, a role can be a concrete manifestation and implementation of a hypothesized identity, presenting an observable product of the self-process. Such role-performance represents *role taking*. A role can also be an observable behavior representing performance by an individual of prescribed, demand behavior determined by a situational context. An individual so performing is *role playing*. The role player is behaving as he feels he is expected to behave, but the behavior does not represent his concept of anything that he believes himself to be in that context. Finally, a role can be an autistically constructed mental behavior, positing and implementing a possible identity hypothesis and representing an unobservable product of the self-process. Such performance is *role figmenting* behavior. The role figmenter often imagines himself as possessing an identity he is aware is not his own as he acts the identity he is imitating. A child playing cowboy knows that he is not actually a cowboy. Daydreaming as well as children's play frequently involves role figmentation.

Roles, therefore, stem from cognitive processes and develop in correlated parallel with the identity assemblage. Both roles and identities are dependent upon cognitive development for their constructions. Role behavior is a cognitive affective process because it is selective, internally organized, and interpreted by relational schema. Thus, roles are not a reflection or reproduction of an association of events from the social world into the individual's response patterns, but are organized and interpreted representations that provide meaning of the world from the individual's ability to place himself into its contexts. Roles provide location and definition of the individual in relation to the world around him.

For roles to be important to the self-process the roles a person takes must bear a functional relationship to his needs, his behavior style attributes, and his system of values. In other words, self-process can be made manifest through identities exemplified in role taking behavior. Role taking behavior provides the individual with an invaluable means for submitting his self-system and its specific hypotheses to tests of reality. For example, values relating to work and productivity that are beginning to appear prior to the adolescent stage are the initiators of certain patterns of behavior that can be defined both as role taking of hypothesized identities and as reality testing of these identities for verification or negation by others.

Roles taken by an individual have their base in his expectations and his perceptions of self for satisfaction of needs that have evolved during the course of development. If the need for security, acceptance, or affiliation has evolved, then taking the role of a warm, accepting person would be one way of satisfying this need. If such a role, when tried, receives reinforcing approval from significant others in the role taker's environment, then that role and the feedback derived from the individual's successful performance substantiate the hypothesized identity represented in the role, and at the same time raise the identity in the identity hierarchy.

Situation Specific Behavior

Since role performance usually occurs in a situational context, in addition to testing a hypothesized identity and elaborating value criteria by processing evaluative feedback from consensus opinions, roles can be situation-specific behavior; that is, an individual may find that the role he takes "works" in one context but not in another. This is part of the individual's social learning process, leading to the knowledge that different identities exemplified in specific roles have to be applied to different situations. Knowledge of role requirements or appropriateness of behavior is part of his social learning, resulting in the ability to select identities for effective and appropriate manifestation in social contexts. The individual, through increasing knowledge of role demands and with an availability of role opportunities, learns to combine identities for social adaptability and for his acceptance as

a member of a social group. A knowledge of role requirements enables an individual to perform role playing or role
taking behaviors in similar situational contexts depending
upon his immediate self needs or his perceptions of others'
demands.

Pervasiveness of Identities

The more general and pervasive an identity becomes, the
greater the number of situations in which it may be successfully used. A pervasive identity becomes interrelated with
other identities and more salient to its relative position in the
identity assemblage. Substantiation provides affective modification to concepts of self and raises an identity in importance to the individual. Resubstantiation in different types
of situations by role taking behaviors acquires multiple
reference loci in the assemblage and enhances self-meaning of
the individual by providing interpretation and definition of
himself across situations as well as in specific contexts.[1]

The operation of values in role selection and performance
must also be examined in relation to roles since the individual's internalized value system is operational in the integration of the identity hierarchy. Since values are involved in
self-process, the roles appropriate to a situation (as defined
in a social and societal framework), if unsatisfying against
the criteria of personal values and their associated needs, will
promote internal conflict. An internal conflict can be manifested in external behavior in various ways, such as
frustration-based aggression or through any of the basic defense mechanisms including withdrawal. Internal cognitive-
affective conflict may lead to identity confusion. Behavior
patterns stemming from internal conflict can become visible
in a youth who experiences social resistance or other difficulties in his attempts to assume adult roles. His expectations
of an adult role and his performance of that role, coupled
with adverse reactions on the part of significant others either
to the manner in which he takes the role or to its premature
assumption, may induce him to cognitively reorganize. He
may react with rebellion, projection, reaction formation, re-

---

[1] The interrelational quality of the identity assemblage provides increased discrimination of self from others by hierarchical integration
and differentiation (Werner 1948) of identity conceptualizations, resulting in enhanced self-meaning.

gression, or other defense mechanisms resulting from his cognitive conflict or dissonance. A complicating factor in role assumption is the inconsistency of situationally defined, demanded, or required behaviors. An individual may successfully take a role one day only to find its enactment forbidden on another, forcing him to reinterpret and reevaluate his previous experiences. Such situational inconsistency is a factor in promoting identity diffusion and role confusion.

When role manifestation of a highly interrelated identity is prevented (i.e., a worker seeking a job), or when it is conceptually denied its existence as a feasible self-perception (i.e., the role of worker by an adult who is unemployable), the seriousness of the result is directly proportional to the pervasiveness of that identity within the identity assemblage. The dissonance result takes the form of a self-disintegration in the sense of a loss of structuring to the assemblage of meanings. Maximal self-disorientation occurs when an identity or cluster of identities once integral with the major part of the assemblage is no longer cognized as a self-reference for maintaining self-meaning.

Once conceptualized as self-hypotheses, identities have to be tested through the assumption of various roles. Resubstantiation of a hypothesized identity or cluster of identities through role behavior lends stability as well as flexibility to the identity assemblage.

Stability of identities over time and flexibility of their exemplification in a multiplicity of roles and contexts result in a continuity of self-meanings despite role variety and changing contextual expectations. However, a constant exemplification of a specific small number of identities and the continuous affirmation gained by their manifestation in specific roles tend to make rigid the identity hierarchy and to limit the adaptability of self-interputations that can be constructed. New concepts of self occasionally must be conceptualized and placed into role taking behavior to maintain an adaptable self-view which is congruent with social and physical changes.

Role Restrictions

With additional maturity the choice of roles becomes increasingly restricted not only by society and the limitations of the individual's physical condition, but also by his value system.

When an individual begins to define and elaborate his values, as they become cognitively-affectively internalized and a basic part of his self-conceptualizations, he curtails the availability of roles. The individual may recognize the alternatives for satisfying needs, but his values prohibit the assumption of roles that are at variance with outcomes dictated by his personally defined code. Thus, the value system interacts with, and to a large extent moulds, the identity hierarchy. Values help to maintain self-consistency despite change in social contexts and their role demands.

Values are restrictive to performance in certain roles and can cause dissonance if these roles are prescribed by an individual's culture as requirements of expected behavior. A person's choice of roles is also limited by the available opportunities for taking the role, the sanctions of society for its performance, his physical conditions, his lack of abilities, and his cognitive orientation or style.

Maturity may be assumed to involve the attainment of complex levels of concept formation and the ability to hypothesize about self and make decisions based on choice. The alternatives are derived from the identities in the identity hierarchy and the array of roles that may be taken to implement the identity selected. Some persons in the process of maturing develop with a very limited conceptualization of alternative solutions. Their cognitive styles preclude the ability to seek multiple means and objectives. They can only envision or hypothesize one solution or path or perhaps a very few, for any choice point in their lives. As a result they persist in the performance of a role, even though the available role prove to be inadequate or unsatisfying to their self-needs. Their inability to seek an alternative role has been obviated by their "constricted" orientation to seek other social opportunities. They can see no other way because they cannot conceptualize another alternative directed toward the same purpose. As a result, they continue to derive negative feedback from their hypothesized identity, instilling a negative self-image, mainly through inappropriate, inadequate, and ineffective role assumption.

As an individual develops and endeavors to implement his self-perceptions in his behavior it is inevitable that in the roles he takes he will encounter many difficulties constituting blocks to optimum self-fulfillment. For example, the adolescent will differ from the adult in the nature of the events in his environment which constitute blocks. The conceptions will overlap considerably but some elements will be present which are characteristically adolescent. This is partly a question of values, and it goes back to those things an adolescent, compared to an adult, considers important and essential in life. In more sociological terms, a description of a cultural category of persons as adolescents must attempt to distinguish between those acts which are characteristic of the category "adolescent" and those characteristic of the various other cultural categories of which the adolescent may be simultaneously a member.

One approach to this difference considers how an adolescent perceives and conditions a role and the identities he exemplifies in an adolescent context in contrast to his behavior in the role in non-adolescent contexts. In one situation he may behave solely in accordance with social expectations and in the other situation he may manifest hypotheses of self for testing in reality contexts. The observable role behavior may or may not be discernible as constituting different self or social dynamics.

Role Confusion

Problems of role definition and role differentiation can become anxiety producing, leading many individuals to present pictures of more or less generalized anxiety. Ausubel (1958) speaks of a state of *transitional anxiety* occurring in the individual during periods of psychological transition. He sees this resulting from threats to self-esteem inherent in a situation in which a person moves from an accustomed state to one on which a new state of equilibrium is sought. The situation of transition may be described as one of aspiration for something yet to be attained.

A desire for independence of self from others leads an individual to assume roles most likely to implement his self-hypotheses. A person often feels "blocked" or "locked into" a role by the behavioral expectations and role requirements of the culture in which he lives. This state constitutes a threat to self-esteem. Such threats to self lead to anxiety and frustration and result in defensive behavior. For most individuals defensive behavior is relatively benign, merely representing an effort on their part to cope within a socially approved framework. But some individuals, as Iannaccaro (1962) notes, attempt to use aggressive, defensive reactions. Some of them will withdraw from the role as a mode of adjustment to frustration rather than compromise themselves.[2]

In many situations a person may perform a role in a manner quite foreign to his own identity concepts. For example, in a given group an individual may have two roles, the role he actually plays in the social context and the role conception he possesses representing his self-needs. The physician who makes his daily rounds, sees patients in his office, and does the myriad jobs of the general practicioner is one example. Those activities are his behavioral requirements for the role of doctor. But these routine behaviors may be very different from the role as he interprets it. He may see himself as a crusader, a white knight in armor combating the forces of evil, a benefactor of mankind. The identity he manifests may be an exemplification of this self-view, modified to accomodate realistic behavioral expectations.

Each individual in social interaction has perceptions of the roles to be performed. He may engage in role playing and role taking behaviors simultaneously or interchangably, depending on his continuous processing of contextual stimulus cues. He may even figment or fantasize a role while performing the expected behaviors demanded by the social act.

If an individual does not encounter reality resistance to his discrepant perceptions of role expectations he may adjust quite comfortably. If reality demands become too difficult he may take refuge in daydreaming or in continuous role figmenting behavior to provide him with meaningful roles that

[2] Schur (1953) explains that anxiety is not in itself pathological, although it may become so if it is too intense. Cameron (1963) notes that anxiety does have useful functions and writes, "It increases a person's readiness for prompt and vigorous action; it adds spice to pleasurable anticipation; it is often the root of laughter and enjoyment. The moderately anxious person, as a watcher, is apt to be more vigilant, cautious and more reaction sensitive to slight stimulation than a complacent one. Moderate anxiety can actually increase endurance during an emergency."

are self-satisfying and self-directed. As a person gains more satisfaction from fantasy and less from reality, he may increasingly resort to dreams and withdraw as much as possible from social participation. Daydreaming is not necessarily morbid; indeed, it is quite normal and healthy. But when it becomes a continual and habitual retreat from reality in the form of social interactions for self-experiences, it is a symptom of serious underlying maladjustment. People who find great satisfaction in daydreaming may find little satisfaction in social transactions. They become increasingly reluctant to seek social experiences as it becomes easier and more self-satisfying to daydream. There is, however, a point of no return which might be called a psychotic shift. This shift occurs when an individual fantasizing his roles completely loses touch with reality. For such a person the roles he creates and assumes in fantasy are no longer imaginary, but are the roles he actually tries to perform in real life.

Factors Influencing Role Performance

If an individual perceives a role forced upon him by social circumstances as congruent with his concepts of self he is able to take the role. If the role is incongruent, he has to role play if he is to assume the role at all. The larger the group the more compartmentalized the available roles and the more restricted an individual becomes in his choice of role behaviors.

Several factors influence a person's placement in a role; the individual can be forced by the group, or he may voluntarily assume and promote the role himself as a way of manifesting his identities. Factors influencing an individual's taking of a role include his level of cognitive development, his personal attributes and abilities, his values, and his relationships with significant others in the compatible or interactive positions he perceives as representing a desired state. In the final analysis, however, the operative factor motivating an individual to take a role is the self-process.

Whatever role a person takes in a group, it is exceedingly important for him even though an observer may consider the role and its consequences trivial and unimportant. A role one person might consider subservient or inconsequential may actually be a great source of satisfaction to its performer as he interprets it in the setting of group responsiveness to his self-hypothesized identity.

Behavior Styles in Roles

Although a social role may be a means for manifesting an identity it is bound to the context in which it is exercised. Social situations have their own demand character in the sense that they set expectancies for those individuals who participate in the situation. Persons who hope to gain acceptance and identity substantiation need to display a certain flexibility in their adoption of social roles and be able to adapt to the different demand characters of different situations. The greater the array of identities an individual incorporates into his identity hierarchy the greater his potential for flexible adaptation. Difficulty arises only when the identity role demanded is in conflict with the individual's value system or when his perception of the appropriate role behavior is faulty. An individual encounters difficulty when his role behavior is perceived by himself as appropriate but is not perceived by others as in accord with social expectations.[3]

During the development of self-concepts and identities an individual learns to assume certain behavior style attributes. These behavior styles characterize him as a person and provide a scientific observer an opportunity to see how a person handles the various roles he takes to implement the identities he selects for use in specific situations. Personality theorists have formulated lists of such attributes, some focused on the inner and some on the outer life of the individual.[4] The

---

[3] With increasing social experiences an individual learns to intersperse role taking and role playing behaviors, enabling him to test identities in specific situations, but to withdraw his self-involvement when his perceptions of the situation change. The reverse also occurs. An individual will behave in accordance with social expectations and, when situations and other persons permit, will manifest an identity in a role, especially in new situations and until he has some stability in his identity assemblage.

[4] Typical of the listings is one proposed by Edwards (1953, 1954). It includes exhibition, autonomy, affiliation, intraception, succorance, dominance, abasement, nurturance, change, endurance, heterosexuality, and aggression.

listing of behavior styles (or personality components) serves little function except as a description of the behavioral attributes exhibited by the role taking process.[5] The value system of each individual sets the criteria for self-evaluation and creates the style of behaviors manifested in the social interchange as satisfying self-needs.

Over time each person works out for himself a behavior style representing these attributes, none of which exist or operate in isolation. Behavior styles develop as an integrated pattern of responses. As a result, clusters or patterns of these attributes occur, consisting of two or more acting in concert. Presumably, for any given situation there are clusters of behavior style attributes which are complementary and lead to integrated behavior and to stability in the identity hierarchy. They are also the means for an individual to assume his own direction and purposive behavior.

Importance of Roles to Self-Process

Roles, as sociological structures, become important for psychological inquiry when the focus is changed from roles and their attendant behaviors to the factors underlying role behavior. Identity concepts are made manifest through available social roles, but it is by postulating role behaviors that we can attempt to differentiate those performances in roles that are intrinsically related to self and those that are divested of self-components. But, it is important to stress that a role itself is not a determiner of the self-meaning of an individual. The social role affords an individual the opportunity to reality test his conceptualizations of self through role taking behavior. Reality, in the form of significant others participating in a social act, provides feedback information to the individual enabling him to modify his concept formations.

From the psychologist's point of view it is expedient to determine not only the normative standards others use for

---

[5] A focus on behavior as an end-in-itself for human behavior results in a reasoning *cul-de-sac*. The observer is unable to determine whether such behavior is manifested identities, demanded performance by others, or unrelated to self-process as activity manifested in the form of reactions to stimulus cues or habit. See Chapter 10 for a further discussion on this point.

evaluation but also to learn about the effects the values, perceptions, and attitudes held by any given individual have upon his concepts of self, his modes of behavior, or conduct, and upon his performance in and assumption of roles.

In a real sense, values and attitudes are an individual not a group matter and the most profitable approach appears to be that of studying each person as a separate developmental entity, considering his own history, needs, adjustments, perceived and available opportunities for self-enhancement, and his choice in role performances.

Self-process has been postulated to be a causal factor for qualifying behavior in roles. To study self and roles it is necessary to differentiate among the three forms of role behaviors for underlying conditions which are related to self-process and those that qualify the involvement of self in behavior.

Chapter 10

Structure of Role Behaviors

IN THE PRECEDING CHAPTERS self-process has been exemplified by an individual's assumption of roles in various forms of role behavior. The distinction between role and role behavior has been made to differentiate between the sociological concept of role and the psychological construct of role behavior.

The basic postulates presented in Chapter 9 delineate the three forms of role behavior as role taking, role playing, and role figmenting. Role taking behavior is a concrete manifestation and implementation of a hypothesized identity, presenting an observable product of the self-process. Role playing behavior is observable behavior representing an individual's performance of behavior prescribed by the demands of a situational context. Thus, role taking behavior represents an implementation of an individual's self-concepts whereas role playing behavior engages him in behavior foreign to his concepts of self. Role figmenting behavior is an autistically constructed mental behavior, positing and implementing a possible identity. In this sense, role figmenting behavior represents an unobservable product of the self-process.

The underlying assumption relating roles and role behaviors is that role behavior consists of those behaviors perceived by an individual as appropriate to the situational demands applied to him as well as those demands imposed upon the situational context by the individual's self-system. The self-system demands represent behavioral outcomes directed by an individual's impulses to achieve certain needs or end states such as goals. Roles afford opportunities for social participation and provide the means for individuals to engage in social acts. The writers assume that through opportunities for social interaction individuals participating in behavioral exchanges can, within the limitations set by their levels of development, make evident conceptualizations of self in their behavior.

Historical Reference to Roles and Self

Sociologists have traditionally referred to specific behaviors in a social context as roles. Social interaction theorists have formulated an interpretation of human behavior as expected social behavior. Social interactionists perceive behavioral expectations as directives of what creates "socialized humanness" with self as a derivative or outcome of the social exchange. This position describes self as a social by-product of interactive conduct. Sociological study of roles and their attendant behaviors are directed toward external societal requirements and specific social opportunities facilitating individuals' adaptation to their social order. Using this theoretical base, roles are social stimuli producing socially desired behavioral responses.

In contrast, the study of self as a process of integrative, interpretive-evaluative concept formation places the emphasis upon the individual and his internal dynamic processes which can produce observable behaviors. This theoretical position focuses on an active individual capable of selectively seeking opportunities for self-definition, self-enhancement, and social adaptation. Thus, self-process is a causal factor in the manifestation of certain role behaviors. Roles can become the means through which an individual exemplifies and assesses his self-process constructions. Roles may be further described as either available social opportunities permitting reality testing of identity concepts, or as demanded social positions requiring an individual to perform in accordance with social expectations.

Traditional Role Concepts

Historically, roles have been defined as positions or status arrangements existing in socially structured organizations.

Divisions of labor within these organizations provide differential structures, for example, levels of responsibility and obligation. By allocating status to structural conditions, roles provide a necessary hierarchy for maintenance and perpetuation of a social organization. Individuals become members of a social group through the assumption and performance of ascribed and socially acceptable aspired roles. Traditionally, an individual's self-meaning was defined, derived, and interpreted by his gradual adoption of roles required for adaptation to the social system. Thus, the historical approach to understanding the development of self was to focus upon overt position and status behaviors as producers of an individual's identity concepts. According to this approach, each individual develops a social identity which is his self-meaning. Such identities develop by appropriate performance of behaviors required by the "generalized others" (Mead 1934). The individual becomes adaptive to his society by reflecting a mirror image of self (Cooley, 1922) by his increasing approximations of becoming what his roles demand and others expect.

The present social-psychological use of role concept has evolved primarily from sociological theory in which patterned behavioral responses are equated with demands of positional interaction. In considering such interaction, sociologists and others who have followed their lead emphasize that response patterns are learned through socialization efforts of others in compatible and interactive relationships.[1]

Social learning of the expectancies of behavior does have an effect on participants in social conduct. However, the variations of behavior evidenced and the motivations for role participation expressed by individuals in social interaction cast doubt upon the adequacy of a unidimensional concept of roles like social learning of required behaviors. The concept of role implies more than the knowledge that certain behaviors are demanded or sanctioned, and that individuals are obligated to conform with socially appropriate responses. An

---

[1] Some reviews of role literature have been presented as summaries of role statements, as clarification of concepts used in role study, and as critiques of role theory as multidimensional constructs. Among these are Biddle and Thomas (1966), Sarbin (1954), Sarbin and Allen (1968), and Jackson (1970).

explanation is needed of the effects of those implicit intra-personal and interpersonal conditions determining how a participant perceives, interprets, and derives meaning from a situational context which permits him to gain and enhance his uniqueness as an individual and to establish a commonality and unity with his social counterparts.

Roles and Effects of Cognitive-Affective Activity

Role expectations and role interpretations have psychological significance since cognitive-affective activity produces the interpretations by processing experiences. Behavior observable in the performance of a role depends upon the meaning an individual derives from perceived situational and self-demands. Interpretations of a role are conditioned by the level of cognitive development attained, as well as by the quantity and quality of previous participation in roles.

Since each person has certain needs and desires relating to and instigated by his perceptions of self, his attempts to satisfy these conditions are essentially idiosyncratic. His concept of others is somewhat variant because he perceives others in contexts dependent on the situational cues to which he attends, and how he processes this information with prior cognitions. He assumes a role by the perceptual-conceptual interpretations he constructs of the situational context, his concept of others, and his concepts of self. He structures meaning in a role that is either demanded of him by others or to one he takes to reality test a self-hypothesized identity.

Roles as Functional to Self-Process

Indicative of the writers' theoretical position that roles are functional to self-process are their observations that some individuals selectively participate or "get involved" in some roles and not in others, withdraw from roles in which they previously participated, and exhibit diverse behaviors in the same role at different times.[2] These observations lend credence to the assumption self-process can be manifested in identities

[2] Chapter 13 presents a research study of illustrative incidents of self and role behaviors.

exemplified by some role behaviors and that these behaviors, because of underlying qualifying conditions, are either appropriate or inappropriate to contextual demands. The importance of roles to self-process redirects the focus to these modifying qualities emanating from or originating within individuals and their concepts of self.

In order to understand the effects of role performance upon facilitation, enhancement, and alteration of self-process, statements postulating implicit conditions conducive to role behaviors affecting the exemplification of self are in need of explication. These postulates stem from a basic premise that role and role behavior are not synonymous concepts but are functionally related. Roles refer to specific ascribed and prescribed behaviors emitted during a social act and are differentially determined by a form of role behavior. Role behavior refers to the methods used by an individual as functions of both observable and unobservable cognitive-affective activity and for enhancing the development of self-as-process. While roles permit social interactions, role behaviors are the means the individual employs to selectively involve himself in his world. Through them he seeks self-evaluation and consensual validation of the identity concepts he has hypothesized for himself.

By theorizing a distinction between roles and role behaviors, some role behaviors may be seen as functional for identities conceptualized by the self-process. Identity concepts are products of cognitive-affective activity producible in observable behavior. They enable an individual to formulate, modify, and validate meanings of his own entity and of himself in concert with others. Identity concepts act as self-references providing self-definition and enabling an individual to locate himself with respect to others. They are the means by which an individual can evaluate himself according to the standards and criteria he has formulated. By them he is able to modify or reaffirm his self-concepts by processing the evaluations others make of him.

Qualifying Conditions in Role Behavior

The underlying conditions for role behaviors are differentially related to self, others, motivation, and reality. Role behaviors are distinguishable by identities, reality bases, locus of control of behavior or source of motivation, perception of situational and contextual demands expected by others, and the cognitive-affective operational level of the individual that affects the processing of inputs resulting from direct and vicarious experiences.

Concept of Others

Chapter 8 presented a brief series of statements on the development and importance of the concept of others in self-process. By developing concepts of others as surrogate representatives of his world, an individual begins to define roles in terms of the surrogates and can anticipate certain behavioral attributes typifying his role stereotypes.

The concept of others has direct relevance to role behaviors for it is through knowledge of others that primary perceptually homogeneous relationships can be cognitively organized, interpreted, and classified as concepts of perceived similarity of self with another. Such concepts are conducive to developing an identification with significant other persons. Others also provide input information which is organized as integrating and differentiating conceptualizations of self from non-self entities.

From other's actions a person becomes familiar with society's demands and the rules he is expected to obey. Others become his social models as he imitates or selectively responds to them during social learning. Through social observation and interaction, an individual sees, hears, emulates, and can fantasize roles. From other's reactions he acquires feedback information as to the appropriateness and effectiveness of his behavior. He reappraises concepts of self by reacting to other's evaluations. Therefore, other persons provide a realistic basis for his values and modify his self-concepts. In doing so, others help to promote decentrism by adjusting egocentric thought constructions toward a mutual perspective.

Role Behavior and Reality

Roles are dependent upon the perception of reality held by individuals involved in interactive behavior. When a role is an inner-constructed condition not consensually validated for expectations and behavioral requirements, then the role becomes a means for non-reality based performance. Roles that have their bases in non-reality criteria are cognitively manufactured in fantasy, imagination, and pretense play. A non-reality basis for role behavior allows the positing of possible, although at times improbable, enactments of figmented concepts of self. In fantasy a person can conceive of himself as anything he wishes without the intervention of reality to control his cognitive constructions. However, with the emergence of propositional thinking, hypothetical deductive reasoning does include reality as a factor. This quality of thinking begins to limit or narrow the range of identity possibilities a person may fancy for himself. Reality, perceived through the interactive effects of others, provides a knowledge of feasibility and acceptability of an individual's self-hypotheses and can supplement his evaluations by the affective feedback he synthesizes from significant others' reactions to his behavior.

Role Behavior and Motivation

Involvement in roles assumes a condition of motivation for the role performance. Motivation for performing or taking a role can be either internally self-reinforced or externally other-reinforced, resulting in different overt behaviors. Intrinsic and extrinsic motivation both refer to the source for determining behavior and are thus the locus of control of a person's behavior.

Locus of control of behavior is a psychological phenomenon,[3] based on the perceptions and interpretations derived by an individual of himself and his actions as a result of his effectiveness in manipulating and controlling his environment. His interpretations of his actions become directives to the quality of his responsiveness to the behavioral expectations he perceives as applicable to him. If he believes he is in control of what happens to him as a result of his actions, then he assesses

[3] Many research studies are addressed to this psychological construct. Of these, the most prominent are a series of studies performed by Rotter (1954).

his conduct in terms of self-defined criteria. If he believes that no matter what he thinks he should do, the outcomes of his behavior are determined by others, or a generalized "other," then he is not responsible to himself for his own actions. This places the locus of control extrinsic to himself. He behaves or performs in accordance with scheduled reinforcement procedures and responds to external criteria for evaluation of his behavior.

Reflexiveness in Role Behaviors

Events and situational cues are selectively perceived by each individual and are processed and interpreted as behavioral requirements affording opportunities for role performances. These expectations qualify manifestations of self in roles by the form of role behavior a person assumes. Feedback gained from behavior is reflexive. Reflexiveness in role behavior is best described as the act of directing an action back upon the doer of the act. Variations of reflexiveness in role behaviors depend on self, others, reality, motivation, and locus of control.

Self-reflexiveness is defined to occur when results of an interaction are directed upon the doer and are integrated into his cognitive structures as affective feedback qualifying concepts of self.

Non-self-reflexiveness occurs when role behavior is only performed in accordance with other's demands. It is interactive but the results of behavior are not encoded as self-related information but as performance evaluation. Hence, the feedback does not immediately qualify concepts of self but relates to performance criteria.[4]

A *non-reflexive* behavior occurs when interaction of self with others lacks reality contexts. A lack of interaction precludes feedback from others concerning self-conceptualizations and occurs primarily in non-reality, fantasized contexts.

---

[4] Knowledge of results of performance (KR) has been studied by Locke and Bryan (1966) and others. Self-reflexiveness does not always result from knowledge of performance results. Unless a *self*-standard has been established prior to the performance, KR is not a sufficient motivator for evaluation of self, although the cognitions of performance results are performance related inputs.

Summary of Conditions

It has been proposed by the writers that roles are differentially related to self, others through reflexiveness, motivation, and the locus of control and reality. In order to understand the structuring of role behaviors, it is relevant to apply these conditional factors to the three forms of role behavior, and to describe the interactive effects of these conditions upon role figmenting, role taking, and role playing behaviors.

Role Figmenting Behavior

Developmentally, the earliest role performance is role figmenting. Role figmenting behavior originates from perceived identity conceptualizations or concepts of self—postulated as possible self-perceptions, lacking a reality base. The conceptualizations are projected in fantasies, daydreams, and imagination. They originate from egocentric perceptions, and also occur in psychotic shifts, psychosis, and autism.[5] The observable behavior accompanying a figmented role assumption may be either appropriate or inappropriate for the situational demands, but the important point is that these external demands are nonperceived or non-attended to by the individual. The behavior results from a subjectively construed, egocentric "reality." Identities are postulated and initiated as intrinsic to a person's own needs or goals and are not related to external environmental demands or restrictions. Motivation is intrinsic and results in self-reinforcement by self-satisfaction, dissatisfaction, or rejection of conceptualizations of possible identities. The role figmenter evaluates a possible identity by standards he has developed in his value system. Role figmenting behavior is not extrinsically motivated by external reinforcements because the external reality accepted by consensus opinion or mutual consent is not a part of the figmenter's selected perceptions at that moment in that con-

[5] A psychotic shift is described in its present usage as a progressive preference for reality detachment occurring when an individual becomes increasingly dependent upon non-reality bases for his cognitive constructions of self, which become almost totally exemplified in fantasized roles.

text. What others demand or reinforce does not determine how the individual perceives his role. Role figmenting behavior is not social interactional and is considered non-reflexive. Figmenting a role is a developmental behavior occurring throughout the life span of individuals, permitting them to posit and hypothesize identities and situations in which external criteria can be temporarily ignored and prevented by choice from altering their standards for self-evaluation.[6]

An exclusive or an overuse of role figmenting results in reality detachment, denoting a pathological shift from a mutually perceived and interpreted reality to a subjectively defined, inner constructed world. Developmentally, infants construct egocentric concepts of self from their own actions and experiences. They react to a subjectively construed egocentric world because they are cognitively unable to perceive and interpret from a decentric view.

Role Taking Behavior

With the development of cognitive operations the allied processes of role taking and role playing occur. As previously indicated, role taking behavior is the manifestation of cognitive-affective constructions of self applied to a situational context. Identities are subjected to the reality of contexts as determined by perceived situational requirements or the demands of environmental agents. The behavior may be appropriate or inappropriate to the perceptions and expectations

---

[6] Some writers describe "play role" situations as rehearsal roles. These roles are described by the present writers as imitative or social learning roles, developed by practicing or repeating prior learned behaviors. They are fundamental to role playing behaviors. However, some individuals use pretense actions to reconstruct the behaviors they have attributed to others. Such behavior is not necessarily based on decentrism nor on the understanding of attitudes, values, or expectations from the other's standpoint (Turner 1956). Instead, this role behavior is based upon an individual construction of what he regards as the attributes of the role in terms of his own criteria, disregarding the context in which he is placed. This role behavior is not involved in a self-other social act, but in a self-imaginary conditional context. Figmented roles are a function of the self-representations an individual constructs of himself at specific moments regardless of the context, others, or reality requirements.

of the observer(s) because role taking behavior is directly a function both of an individual's *self* system needs and of his perceptions of the expectations set by contextual requirements. The identities are intrinsically derived by hypotheses from the self-process and are evaluated by values ascribed as self-standards or criteria.

Role taking is self-reflexive. Identities become modified or confirmed as self-references by processing of feedback from social interaction and from the individual's own evaluation of his behavior. His motivation is intrinsic, initiated by self-exemplary needs, and self-reinforced. Feedback results in modification or enhancement of cognitive structures by attaching affect and is reflected in the person's self-evaluation by effects of the conceptualized identity in action. The locus of control for role taking behavior is located within the individual. Reality promotes the social learning process, as socialization, and eventually modifies the "all things are possible for myself" attitudes. By the intervention of reality with self-reflexiveness the individual learns to determine the probability that some identities are more likely or appropriate as self-definitions and self-representations than are others and are more probable of gaining acceptance and substantiation from significant others or from reference groups to which he adapts.

Role Playing Behavior

As role taking develops, another form of role behavior is simultaneously emerging. This form of role behavior, called role playing behavior, is also a function of cognitive development. Role playing is reality based upon situational or environmental expectations or demands, but feedback from performance or enactments, in the form of affect, is not processed in the self-system because concepts of self are not involved in the role playing behaviors. Anti-identities, those identities not conceptualized by the individual of himself at that moment in that context or those concepts not attributed to him by his own interpretations, are the ones he overtly performs. The performances are behavioral demands of required, ascribed, or prescribed expectations as determined by external criteria. The external demands of the social act are not related to the self-system demands of his self-exemplary needs. Role playing behavior is extrinsically motivated, externally reinforced, and evaluated. The results of the evaluations do not affect the identity structures. With maturity and stability of self-meaning, however, an individual's value system is increasingly applied to self in such a manner as to prevent his performance in certain available roles. Role playing behavior is evaluated by performance criteria and not as substantiation or negation of self-hypothesized identities as in role taking behavior.

Locus of control of behavior is external to the individual, imposed upon him in the forms of sanctions, proscriptions, and behavioral demands. Although role playing is non-self-reflexive, knowledge of results of performance effectiveness and appropriateness are cognitively encoded. In this manner, cognitive dissonance may alter previous cognitions and change a concept of self by reassessment of the anti-identity. Reassessment of an anti-identity may in turn cause a reformulation of concepts by generating new interpretations or by including aspects of the anti-identity to be postulated as possible self-hypotheses. At some point in time, an individual may assume a role taking behavior and test the newly hypothesized identity in a situational context for affirmation or refutation of a self-perception. This occurs when affect has been encoded, modifying previous cognitions with the result that new meanings of self may be conceptualized.

Role Behavior Interchangeability

Although the forms of role behavior are discrete, an individual's role behavior at any time may represent any one of the role forms or any combination of them. To the observer the behavior may be indistinguishable except by his perceptions of appropriateness of the role response and by the performer's adaptability to social role expectations and demands. However, a given role performance may be assumed to refer to the self-process if it can be posited as an outcome of self-evaluation together with a cognitive-affective structuring of stimulus inputs as relevant to the individual's self-perceptions and conceptions.

Role behavior interchangeability frequently occurs as a result of social conformity. Role playing behavior is the manifestation by the individual of anti-identities. When the person receives external reinforcements for these anti-identities, he assimilates into his cognitive structures the results of his actions. In evaluating his own performance, if he can relate parts of the anti-identity by cognitively *integrating* aspects of the anti-identity to *differentiate* new concepts in terms of his self-needs and values, he is able to *formulate* new identities. These new identities can be role taken when a context permits their manifestation. Since role playing behavior involves cognition, by producing behavior at variance with self-percepts, it follows that cognitive dissonance (Festinger, 1957) or cognitive strain (Sarbin and Allen, 1968) will often ensue. In the event dissonance does occur, it may be eliminated or reduced by abstracting, accepting, or reorganizing an anti-identity as a possible self-representation. When this occurs, role taking behavior replaces role playing.

An individual can deny relationship to the anti-identity by evaluating external demands and reinforcements. If expectations are not congruent with a person's value system, the anti-identity is discarded as a possible self-hypothesis and may continue to be performed as role playing behavior fulfilling the criteria of external contexts. The individual disregards or discounts the external reinforcements of his performance as non-consequential to his conceptions of self. With further development, refinement, and elaboration of his values, some role playing behaviors at variance with his standards for modes of conduct will be rejected. He will either withdraw altogether from the context demanding the role or impose his self-criteria on the context by role taking, representing himself as he cognitively-affectively perceives himself.

Effects of Role Taking Behavior on the Identity Assemblage

Constant external reinforcement can affect structuring in the identity hierarchy. If an identity held by an individual is given positive reinforcement, that is, if it is substantiated by others each time it appears, the identity will be elevated in importance within the assemblage of identities and interrelated with other identities and roles. The change in salient position of an identity occurs as an attempt by the individual to alleviate any discrepancy created by the way he perceives the importance of the identity with respect to his values and needs, and how others perceive the value of his behavior. Many of the intrapositional changes within the assemblage occur during periods of transition in which certain role performance, expressing concepts of self, are no longer acceptable to others nor to the individual's own needs and values.[7]

At this point, it is well to summarize several basic premises for the study of self and role behavior. First, identities are posited as cognitive constructions and, as such, involve the possession of identities and assemblage of identities on the part of a human as a self-perceiving organism. Second, a self-perceiving organism's state of cognitive developmental maturity is central for an understanding of the interpretations an individual makes of the demands placed upon him. Third, the assumption of the observer that the self-perceiving human organism is capable of understanding a consensus perception of reality; he is capable of decentring his own viewpoint. And, finally, the importance of the quality of mental processes that the self-perceiving individual has at his disposal for restructuring cognitions by inputs and feedback from experiences. Furthermore, values are developmentally constructed and progress in their complexity and applicability by ascribing standards, specifying rules, or establishing criteria for modes of behavior (conduct) and end states of existence. These criteria, when applied to the self-process, become functional as evaluating self-concepts and for determining behavior styles evidenced by the individual in his strivings and directionality, and in specific social interactions.

Conditions for Role Behavior

Although each condition for role behavior is necessary, no one condition is sufficient of itself to create a specific quality of role behavior. However, as conditional factors change, the quality of role behavior changes to another form. Table I

[7] These transition periods are well documented in psychological and sociological literature. Among these, the most obvious are the adolescent period, the psychological-sociological changes from work to retirement, or the problems in transition from school to work conditions.

TABLE 1 Conditions for Role Behavior

Role Behavior	Reflexive	Motivation	Reality	Identity Base
Role Taking	Yes—Interactive Self-Other-Self	Intrinsic; locus of control—Self	Yes—Consensus mutually perceived	Self concepts-Identity concepts manifested in contexts
Role Figmenting	No—Not Interactive	Intrinsic; locus of control—Self	Non-reality subjectively	Self concepts-Identities not in context
Role Playing	Interactive but non-reflexive to self structure—Related to performance	Extrinsic; locus of control—Others	Yes—Consensus mutually perceived	Anti-identities, contextual derivations of behavior
Role Taking	Yes—Interactive Self-Other Self	Intrinsic; locus of control—Self	Yes—Consensus mutually perceived	Self concepts-Identity concepts manifested in contexts

Note: As conditional factors change, the form of role behavior changes to either one above or below it in this table.

illustrates the interrelation of role behaviors and their modifying conditions.

The two more primary factors are an identity base and a reality base. Interdependent with the identity base is motivation-locus of control, and interdependent with reality is reflexiveness. These latter modifiers of the primary factors qualify role behavior. Since identity concepts and perception of reality emanate from cognitive-affective processes, the latter is fundamental to this theory.

Summary of Role Behavior Postulates and Corollaries

The first postulate and its corollaries relate to role taking behavior.

> *Postulate I.* A role can be a concrete manifestation of a hypothesized identity or set of identities presenting an observable product of the self-process.
>
>> *Corollary 1* A role taking behavior is intrinsically motivated with locus of control of behavior assumed to reside within an individual.
>>
>> *Corollary 2* A role taking behavior is reality based and the results of the manifestations of behavior are processed as feedback and are reflexive to the self-assemblage.
>>
>>> *Corollary 2.1* A role taking behavior is reflexive, and is related to both self-demands and to demands of the situational contexts.
>>
>> *Corollary 3* Role taking behavior can change into other qualities of role behavior if certain conditional factors, such as differential relation to self, motivation, reality, or reflexiveness, change their direction.

The second postulate and its corollaries relate to role playing behavior.

> *Postulate II.* A role can be an observable behavior representing performance by the individual of prescribed, demanded, or expected behaviors as determined by situational contexts.
>
>> *Corollary 1* A role playing behavior is extrinsically motivated with the locus of control of behavior assumed to reside in others.

Corollary 1.1   A role playing behavior is the manifestation of those aspects of performance demanded by others as appropriate for the context.

Corollary 2   A role playing behavior is a manifestation of anti-identities not derived from cognitively organized concepts of self.

Corollary 2.1   Anti-identities are cognized as demanded behavioral enactments necessary for functional effectiveness, satisfying perceived external demands.

Corollary 3   Role playing behavior is reality based, interactional but not reflexive to self-structures. The results of the manifestations of behavior are evaluated as performance criteria and not as evaluation of hypothesized identity concepts.

Corollary 4   A role playing behavior can change into other qualities of role behavior if certain conditional factors change, that is, if self, motivation, locus of control, or reflexiveness change their directions.

The third postulate of role behavior and its corollaries relate to role figmenting behavior.

Postulate III.   A role can be an autistically constructed mental behavior, positing and implementing a possible identity or set of identities, representing an unobservable product of the self-process.

Corollary 1   A role figmenting behavior is a mental construction of a possible identity or set of identity concepts, intrinsically motivated, with locus of control of behavior assumed to reside within the individual.

Corollary 2   A role figmenting behavior is non-reality based, and external feedback is inconsequential since others are not cognized as basic for substantiation of cognitive self-constructions.

Corollary 2.1   A role figmenting behavior is nonreflexive to self-structures due to its lack of social interaction.

Corollary 3   A role figmenting behavior can change to other qualities of role behavior if certain conditional factors become differentially related to self, motivation, locus of control, reality or reflexiveness.

Summary of Structure of Role Behavior

Roles permit a person to organize, identify, define, hypothesize, and test concepts of self in social reality and in his idiosyncratic thought processes. In egocentric thought man does not test himself in relation to others but solely against internal criteria. If evaluations by others have no access to his cognitions, he develops autistically and cannot accept other perceptions and expectations as part of his self-evaluations. Without reality and a reflexive nature of role, an individual cannot fit into a predictable social unit because he cannot learn to modify his behavior in keeping with social expectations or sociocultural norms.

Reflexiveness, intrinsic-extrinsic motivation, and reality components of role have strong impact on the reasons for role enactment as they relate to self and society. Since each person is an individual, his cognitive-affective structures, developed by his own actions and reactions on his environments, are idiosyncratic. Each person develops his own cognitions and meanings of self, but a commonality is evidenced in his behavior and in others who share his interactions in compatible or similar roles. A common base of culturally prescribed behavioral and attitudinal expectations in the form of shared experiences and demand roles provides a social regularity to role behavior. Observable differences may appear in the manner each person interprets situations and behaviors. But the commonality that exists in social expectations lends a degree of predictability to what each person expects in a social interchange. These behavioral expectations enable him to postulate concepts of self as self-hypotheses for consensus opinion and for self-evaluation of the results of his own role behavior.

Chapter 11

Self-Esteem and Responsibility

ONCE A PERSON ACQUIRES A SYSTEM OF VALUES and builds an integrated set of reality-tested self-concepts, what value does he place upon the self he conceptualizes? What is the self-esteem status of an individual at various crucial periods in his construction and integration of his self-concepts? These are important questions for the understanding of the behavioral dynamics of any given individual. They are particularly crucial for a psychologist who assumes a therapeutic or counseling relationship with an individual, whether child, adolescent, or adult. A great many of an individual's decisions rest upon his evaluation of his hypothesized identities as well as upon his overall evaluation of himself.

Developmental Aspects of Self-Esteem

During his first ten years of life, an individual's problems of self-esteem tend to be structurally simple. Most children with their concrete approach to their experiences accept what they perceive as the evaluation of the significant figures in their lives. Much of their self-evaluation rests upon whether or not they are obeying the rules for conduct laid down by these figures. A problem arises when the opinions of significant figures appear in disagreement, or when a person particularly important in their lives appears inconsistent in his opinions and rules. During the early period of negativism, the first real attempts at self-assertion which often bring a child in conflict with his significant figures may cause a problem. But, for the most part, the normally reared child will have relatively few problems in this area and his self-esteem status will be relatively high. Young children have not reached a cognitive development, nor have they usually had sufficient experience, to question themselves. The typical question of doubt rather takes a form such as, "Mommy, do you love me?"

The state of an adolescent, as he enters the period of formal operations and widens his experiences, is much more complicated and self-questioning. Adolescents are more insecure than children. Their concepts of self are being modified, and they are more analytic not only about themselves but about the world in general. An adolescent has many self-decisions to make, many of which seem to him literally earthshaking in their consequences. He has to make an occupational or curricular choice and has to decide whether he is good enough to do what must be done to succeed in a given occupation. He has to decide whether he has the ability to participate in various social or athletic enterprises. Heterosexually, is he attractive enough to interest and succeed with a really desirable member of the opposite sex? Is he a good son, is he the kind of person others like? Will he succeed in marriage? Will he make a good parent? Does he feel he has the courage, moral and physical, to carry out his convictions and those tasks and roles that have been assigned to him? Is he a coward? Does he have stamina? Could he visualize himself as a leader?

An adult's problems of self-esteem are simpler than those of an adolescent. Maturity stabilizes self-concepts and provides a more firm picture of self. An adult has tested reality upon many occasions and gained a self-view based upon a long experience of identity formation and role assumption. He is more self-accepting and less self-critical than an adolescent. Unfortunately, he is also typically less idealistic. His self-expectations have been tempered by experience and some perspective of the relative importance of what goes on in his world. If he has developed normally, he has learned to cope with many of his own self-deficiencies and to emphasize optimally those self-aspects that are strongest. Of course, not all chronological adults have left their adolescence behind; a number continue to operate throughout the years of their maturity as if they were teenagers. These retarded adults encounter the greatest problems of self-esteem in their maturing years as they still continue to battle reality.

In late maturity and in old age the self-esteem problem again arises. New problems and roles result from the process of aging and from the view of the aged held by the more youthful contributing society. Menopause, retirement, and increasing physical disability are problems for which the aging person, as he enters his declining years, must work out coping behavior. Fortuitous circumstances, such as the loss of a loved one, or of a job, or the occurrence of an unexpected and difficult circumstance can also cause self-view crises during the adult years. This becomes particularly true if there are valid reasons for self-blame.

No mention has been made of the special problems of self-esteem of any individual in society who faces discrimination or other culture-based sanction. These can become problematic to the exemplification of self as an individual's self-concepts continually find rejection in society's non-acceptance of the roles by means of which he attempts to implement his self-concepts and his hypothesized identities.[1]

Constitution of Self-Attitudes

As Rosenberg (1965) writes, "When an individual is faced with a serious and urgent decision, and when a major basis for this decision is his view of what he is like, then the self-image is

---

[1] The question could be asked how, under circumstances of rejection, a discriminated against minority group member could build a structure of self-concepts permitting any appreciable degree of self-esteem. The answer is that a minority group member does receive the reinforcement of approval from his own subculture and from his references groups; it is also probable that his experiences in the general culture may not be universally adverse. A minority group member may construct many reasons to reject the validity of the view attributed to him by the general culture. In any event, there is no reason to assume the inevitability of low self-esteem in all or in most members of discriminated against minority groups.

Special problems arise when an individual with high self-esteem is suddenly faced with societal non-acceptance. Deliberate programs of dehumanization, such as those perpetrated in Nazi concentration camps during the 1930s and early 1940s, succeeded in the destruction of the self-esteem of large numbers of persons. But even there, as Frankl (1959) and others have indicated, some were able to resist the negative feedback.

likely to move to the forefront of his attention." Rosenberg further notes that people have attitudes which they apply toward objects and the self may be thought of as a developing process toward which one has an attitude. "There is no qualitative difference in the characteristics of attitudes toward the self and attitudes toward soup, soap, cereal, or suburbia." Drawing upon the formulations of Krech and Crutchfield (1948), and Newcomb (1950), Rosenberg notes that attitudes differ in content, direction, intensity, importance, salience, consistency, stability, and clarity, and that individuals' self-classifications are made on the basis of these eight dimensions.

We might look at these eight in terms of any given individual's self-attitude. Where *content* is concerned, what does a person see when he looks at himself? This might include his sex, religion, attributes, school status, skills, and physical structure. Where *direction* is concerned, how favorable or unfavorable, positive or negative, are his feelings toward himself? *Intensity* relates to the strength of his self-feelings—he may feel strongly adverse to himself, or only mildly so. *Salience* of self-attitude is indicated by the amount of time and effort the individual expends considering himself, his characteristics, and attributes in comparison to other things he does. *Importance* is indicated by how important the person feels he is compared to other aspects of his environment. *Stability* is determined by the extent to which the individual's self-attitudes fluctuate over time, while *consistency*, closely related to stability, depends upon how contradictory the fluctuating self-attitude may be. Finally, *clarity* is determined by the extent to which the self-attitudes are sharp and well defined. For example, an individual's self-esteem may stem from his upper socioeconomic status; he may feel strongly favorable to himself and spend a great deal of time thinking of himself, always in clear and unambiguous terms, as an exceedingly important person compared to anyone else he knows.

The normally developing person whether his self-attitude is favorable or unfavorable, usually feels that he is an important person, worthy of a great deal of his own (as well as everyone else's) attention. If environmental circumstances and personal attributes are favorable, the self-view is generally positive rather than negative. As Rosenberg (1965) states, "The distinctive characteristic of self-attitudes . . . is that everyone is motivated to hold the same attitude toward the object, namely, a positive attitude." Murphy (1947) writes, "The main self attitudes, those involving the fear of losing the self esteem . . . struggle to keep the self picture good." The adolescent typically filters out, ignores, or resists exceptions to the favorable self-postulates he holds. Murphy further notes, "The self-picture is carried about and consolidated until the individual feels that ordinarily it will hold up pretty well against the efforts of others to penetrate or disvalue it. Any effort of others gradually to dissect or belittle it is handled with reasonable dispatch by taking countermeasures." When the self-attitudes do become unfavorable the results in the whole adjustive picture presented by the person may be quite serious. Rubens (1965) notes that disturbances in the development of self-idealization and in maturational development of the self tend to produce the following five adverse behavior tendencies in older youth:

1 Extreme intensity and shifting fluidity of clinical phenomena
2 Intensification of pre-existing attitudinal and emotional conflicts
3 Changeableness and tentativeness of solutions in such conflicts
4 Confusion in the self-concept and identity confusion
5 Tendency toward exaggerated self-idealization

Rubin's fifth behavior tendency is related to Murphy's characterization of the individual's effort to keep the self-picture good.

Self-Definition

The answer to the question "Who am I?" often provides insight into the structuring of an individual's identity hierarchy. There are, of course, vast individual differences in people's answers, but a normative developmental trend is observable. Using 1185 subjects aged seven to twenty-four, Kuhn (1960) reports that the older an individual is the more he is apt to define himself in terms of social group membership role definition and categories such as educational attainment, age, and sex. Females tend to identify themselves more by sex and kinship than do males. Persons who embark upon or contemplate professional training tend to mention this affiliation early in their responses. In a study contrasting self-perceptions of males and females, Rongved (1961) reports that women select characteristics emphasizing motivational forces while males show a preference for descriptive words depicting regulatory activity. However, sex differences for motivational tendencies decrease with age and those for regulating qualities increase.

One of the tasks of growing up is to develop self-concepts which allow ease in taking the roles set by biological and physical makeup. Growing up also involves the ability to play certain roles expected in the culture in which one is reared. One of the most important of these roles involves acceptance of masculinity for boys and of femininity for girls. The ability to accept and play appropriate "demand" roles appears to be a result of an individual's personal adaptability and emotional stability. This view was confirmed in a study by Mussen (1961) in which he reports that adolescent boys who scored highest on the masculinity-femininity scale of the Strong Vocational Interest Blank showed greater indications of personal adequacy and emotional stability than did boys who scored lowest.

The same situations hold true in other areas. For example, Perkins and Shannon (1965) report that ideal self-scores are related to both I.Q. and academic success. Pilisuk (1962) reports that self-evaluations (defined as attitudes closest to one's conception of oneself) changed in adolescents during high school in accordance with their level of performance in school.

Self-Continuity

That changes bring differences is a trite but true aphorism and this fact presents problems during the development of self-concepts. Even within an individual what is today may not be tomorrow, to the point of losing continuity with oneself. An adult whose identity has become relatively secure can rationalize this lack of continuity, but the adolescent whose identity hierarchy is at best insecure due to lack of substantiation of self-hypothesis in roles has more difficulty. He has trouble maintaining continuity with himself and recognizing himself as he was in the past as the same person he now is. The tendency is to allow a generalized term to stand for the continuity and say, *"Then* I was a child, *now* I am grown up." But one is not a child one day and a grown-up the next. There are years of transition and living in between, so that the generalized response answers nothing. So often in a clinic an adolescent will say, "I don't know what is the matter with me. I never used to be like that. What has happened to me?"

Although self-process is still developing, continuity and the security it brings are needed; self-meaning becomes increasingly stable since the adolescent resents changes and clings to what he has built. He structures his identity hierarchy, allotting certain identities greater importance in specific evaluations. This is particularly true when the resolution of hypothesized identities has been satisfactory as they are confirmed by experiences and offer an acceptable self-view. Engel (1959) notes the relative stability of self-concepts during the adolescence of better adjusted children. Over a two-year period she found that those with "a positive self-concept" retained this status, but those whose original self-concepts were negative displayed less stability over the two years.

Hypothesized identities are less stable during these same years, but they too begin to display considerable stability. The relationship between self-meaning and identities causing stability in one leads to stability in the other, the premise being that identities are tested and evaluated and either will be incorporated or discarded from the hierarchy. Therefore, those identities that are not stable have a greater probability of being discarded and revised in different identity clusters, but do not disturb the basic hierarchy structure. Lecky (1945) emphasizes that a developed self-symbol is quite resistant to change, the current concept being the one the individual strives to maintain even if he has to resort to defensive behavior.

Change and rearrangement have been described as complex tasks, with floundering and defense mechanisms appearing until a hierarchy is achieved. This hierarchy is, to a large extent, molded by the values of the individual. Satisfying self-needs the values create is accomplished by striving for desirable goals. These goals are both personally and culturally evaluated and must be acceptable to both the individual and his society if equilibrium is to result. Efforts by teachers, parents, and society in general to impose various standards incongruent with self-concepts are bound to meet resistance and defensive behavior, particularly if the peer culture is supportive and passivity has not already been built into the child by previous child-rearing practices.

Combs and Snygg (1959), commenting on resistance to change, write, "The stability of the phenomenal self makes change difficult by causing us (a) to ignore aspects of our experience which are inconsistent with it, or (b) to select perceptions in such a way as to confirm the concepts of self we already possess." They feel that change in perceived self depends upon three factors: the clarity of experience provided by a new perception, the way the revised concepts fit into the existing self-organization, and the relation of the revised concepts to the individual's needs. Obviously, less important aspects of self-concepts are more susceptible to change than are more central ones. Still, changes come slowly unless the experience that includes change is particularly vivid. An individual who feels inadequate in any situation is hardly likely to feel suddenly adequate on the basis of a single success experience.

Antecedents of Self-Esteem

As studies by Searles (1966), Fine and Jennings (1965), and Cernik and Thompson (1966) attest, the circumstances in which a child is reared are exceedingly important to his identity hierarchy and to his self-esteem. Elkin (1958) points to the primacy of the family setting and parental child-rearing practices in the development of the sort of person who emerges. Cernik and Thompson (1966) report that adolescents most successful in recognizing their own strengths and weaknesses presented a pattern of objectivity, organization, positive approach, and a tendency to utilize home resources. Parents appear to be the key figures in the home's influence. Medinnes (1965) notes that adolescent self-regard was more closely related to the mother's child-rearing attitudes than to the father's. Dignan's (1965) study supports Erikson's theory that, of the early single identifications, that with the mother is extremely significant for identity formation during adolescence.

Coopersmith (1967) studied, over a period of eight years, the antecedents and consequences of self-esteem in terms of background factors, personal characteristics, and the parental treatment associated with high, medium, low, and defensive self-esteem. He asked his subjects, "What are the conditions that lead an individual to value himself and to regard himself as an object of worth?" The answers were: parental warmth, clearly defined limits, and respectful treatment. These three response clusters supply affective feedback to the child's cognitive system during the process of structuring the information derived from interactions. Coopersmith's opinion was that the four best ways of altering an individual's self-esteem in a positive direction are successes, inculcation of ideals, encouragement of the individual's aspirations, and help in building defenses against onslaughts on self-perception.

Self-Responsibility

A major developmental task is the attainment of a sense of responsibility if the individual is to become a socially useful person and of maximum use to himself. There are in actuality two quite different kinds of responsibility. The more basic of the two is *interior responsibility* which involves accepting responsibility for himself in the sense that he should take care of himself, be self-dependent, and assume the responsibility for becoming the person he conceives himself to be. Interior responsibility represents the implementation of a kind of caretaker drive. Interior responsibility involves an individual's accepting a dependence upon himself for being consistent with self-concepts. A behavioral counterpart of interior responsibility is manipulation and competence, resulting in mastery.

The other, the more obvious, is exterior responsibility. This type of responsibility involves a sense of relatedness to others and an accountability to others or institutions. It consists partly in taking upon oneself the function of seeing that something gets done and done well, and it is obviously an attribute of leadership. It leads to the role of the instigator, the mover. Exterior responsibility implies involvement and may have as its origin either extrinsic or intrinsic motivation. It is either externally initiated and reinforced or self-initiated and reinforced. Intrinsically motivated exterior responsibility represents the identity assemblage or the developing self-concepts through behavior style or modes of conduct exhibited by the individual. These behaviors are determined to a great extent by the self-exemplary needs and value system. The intrinsically motivated exterior responsible person exemplifies his identities in responsibility roles through role taking behaviors. The intrinsically motivated person is usually typified as self-actualizing or self-fulfilling of self-expectations.

Extrinsically motivated exterior responsibility is a behavior style that eventually results in self-aggrandizement in social settings. It is the means by which a person gains social approval and achieves social conformity in his conduct. The person who is extrinsically motivated in his responsibility for others initially engages in role playing by fulfilling social expectations of his behavior and gains feedback as to the adequacy of his performances.

A person's perception of his functional effectiveness must be cognitively-affectively assessed. For an individual to perceive himself as a responsible person, he must achieve a relative degree of autonomy, represented by a belief that he is independent and separated from other's control of his actions and conduct. He perceives himself as the initiator of his actions. However, autonomy is a relative condition and must be personally defined.

Some persons appear to be independently capable of performing and coping with tasks. They appear to possess autonomy in a behavioral sense, but upon investigation are performing prescribed tasks. They do not have a freedom of choice about how they prefer to respond. Others appear to be autonomous but are responding because of basic needs or compulsions. Some are confined or bound to a subculture in which they lack broad cultural experiences, limiting their possibility for conceiving alternatives for their actions. Their subcultures can be constrictive to experiential possibilities and confine role choices, thereby limiting the variety of conditions available for testing identities and for developing a self-other responsibility.

The concept of responsibility is basic to the progress of civilization and can be related to many aspects of psychic performance, including creativity. As responsibility declines, people become more irresponsible, more selfish or self-centered, more hedonistic, more prone to crime, and less self-dependent. Responsibility for one's actions and the results of one's behavior is related to self-responsibility. Commitment or involvement in social problems can only reflect a responsibility for the self if the individual believes he is the determiner of the cause and results of his actions. Lack of responsibility is a social as well as a personal disorder. The closing years of the Roman Empire knew it well. Modern writers such as Wheelis (1958) and McLuhan (1964) have described its symptoms in our times.

Self-Esteem and Responsibility

It is reasonable to postulate a high degree of relationship between responsibility and self-esteem. The taking of responsibility either for oneself or for others indicates the possession of enough personal confidence and self-security to enable an individual to be willing to risk taking a responsibility role.[2] One would not expect a person whose tests of reality had been unsuccessful and who had behind him a long history of personal and social failure to assume responsibility for himself or for anyone else. For such a person, identities expressed in responsibility-taking roles would either be lacking from or exceedingly low in the identity hierarchy of his self-conceptual system. Responsibility taking is, of course, a vital aspect of an individual's value system. Value reeducation is the best approach to the inculcation of responsibility in rearing children. Such value emphasis might well serve to raise responsibility-taking to a higher rank in an individual's identity hierarchy, particularly when opportunity may also be offered for some successful responsibility role assumptions.

---

[2] It is unlikely that an insecure person of low self-esteem would attempt to play a responsibility-taking role even when situational expectations and demands would strongly indicate the necessity of a responsibility role assumption. Such a person, however, might figment a responsibility role, particularly if his system of values placed a positive value upon the assumption of responsibility.

Chapter 12

Therapy and Self-Insight

THE PREVIOUS CHAPTERS DEAL WITH THE NATURE OF self and the developmental manner in which an individual builds, rebuilds, revises, and finally integrates concepts of self. Self-concepts constitute an individual's means of viewing himself and the surrounding world. He interprets his environment and the people in it in the light of his self-conceptions, and his problem solving and role behavior is based upon and limited by these same concepts of self. The insights he has are mediated by his self-process and he tests reality in terms of the image he has drawn of himself.

A difficult problem arises when particularly stringent reality forces a person to reexamine and modify his self-concepts when modification seems impossible, when the results of self-examination are traumatic, or when the sheer act of embarking on self-examination seems too much to face. Some individuals possess enough self-security or enough coping ability to handle this problem, at least to some extent, on their own. But others are unable to face the tasks of self-examination and modification either efficiently or without harm to themselves in the absence of therapeutic assistance or intervention. Optimally, such intervention has the function of self-change through the inculcation of new insights.

Insight as Restructuring

When the therapist speaks of inculcating insight, he means changing one insight for another, or replacing one insight no longer held tolerable with another. But this means changing self-concepts involving a restructuring of the interacting identity hierarchy and value system and, of course, a change in their manifestations in attitudes and role behaviors. Unfortunately, the older one becomes the more difficult it is to effect these changes; concepts of self are not only habituated, they are also a product of the emotions as well as of the intellect. Man's undoubted ability, at least to a point, to increase in problem solving and cognitive ability through the early and middle decades of his life always has the brake of the functionally more primitive emotions. Freud said that in our self-construction we build a house of cards and that the edifice may be blown down, but Boenheim[1] notes that the house becomes, with increasing age, a house of concrete blocks. Sometimes the therapist is able to make revisions without bringing the house down by showing the client how reality can be viewed in terms of the self he already has, and that it can be coped with and understood in these terms. One might say that the problem is that of redecorating the house rather than in bringing it down. Of course, as was mentioned earlier, an individual may attempt his own readjustment or refurnishing without therapeutic assistance. He may well be successful, although such a procedure tends to be fortuitous rather than deliberate and is probably continuous, at least to some extent, in nearly everyone. But, when the whole house that represents an individual's construction of himself, and through him of the world, must come entirely down, then therapeutic assistance is a necessity.

Insight as Self-Hypothesis

Handling this problem conceptually is difficult because insight is only a hypothesis. Acting on his self-concepts the client would hypothesize that he has insight, while the therapist would insist that this insight must be replaced by his own insight, or that the client's insight must be at least revised in terms of his own. Here we have a battle of hypotheses with the client using his arsenal of mental mechanisms to defend his hypotheses but, by means of transference, gradually giving

[1] Personal communication.

ground. In this sense, transference becomes a holding operation acting as a substitute for insight while the client gropes
for new insight. Transference is largely a form of self-
exteriorization. Of course, the client who voluntarily comes
to the therapist shows that he has reason to question his
hypotheses and so may present an easier problem. The greater
problem is presented by the person who enters therapy under
pressure with the viewpoint that nothing is wrong; and, for
society, the ultimate problem is posed by the person who does
not seek help at all.

The inculcation of new insight requires the client to build
new concepts of self and successfully test them against reality
to find that they are congruent with his past and present experiences as he now interpets them, and also with his expectations of the future. Further, the client must be taught new
coping behavior in the form of role taking in terms of his new
concepts of self. The change is great, and combating it are
all of the reinforcements and rationalizations of the past. The
client must hypothesize a future in which he has certain expectations and must find a way of relating his self-structure
to these expectations. One can not look back, but must look
ahead if a cure is to be effected. Thus coping behavior, an
expectation of the future, and confidence in the adequacy of
the coping behavior to meet the demands of the future are
important. Therapy should engender both security and confidence in the future. The essence of this security is the
individual's possession of a conviction that he can cope with
what is going to happen.

Multiple Nature of Insight

An all-or-none simplification of the unitary nature of insight
is not intended by this discussion. All individuals possess
many insights involving different events and spheres of the
individual's activities and identities as a person. Many of these
insights are only partial and are certainly never consciously
examined. Yet they are all related to some degree, and to
change one is to change the whole matrix of relationships.
Perhaps the success, or the probability of success, of therapy
depends on how serious the matrix of changes will be. Obviously a new insight, whose matrix relationships are still

undefined, will be more easily manipulated by the therapist than will a long existing insight with strong and well-defined relationships among the individual's whole structure of insights. Insight is not always effective because too many different insights are involved and the attack is only partial to that point. An individual does not move with equal ease among all his identities. Correspondingly, insight in therapy may come quickly and with complete effect since the insight being replaced is new and has relatively few affiliations.

A difficult consideration for the outside observer, relevant to a decision about the advisability of therapy is the adequacy of the self-view of the individual in question. He can be judged only by the maladaptiveness of his role taking or the behavioral ramifications of his role playing; the self-structure and self-percepts underlying these roles are difficult to manipulate, especially because they are not always in the conscious realm of the person. There is also the question of how far and under what circumstances self-insight should be forced.

The foregoing discussion of therapy and insight has assumed that self-insight is an outcome of a person's self-meaning and that one way of examining the adequacy of a self is to examine the reality base of the insight, for certainly one may have a false self-view. But when the possibility of false insight is posited, is there not a contradiction in terms? Is it possible to have false self-insight? The answer is yes if insight is characterized as a hypothesis. Presumably the individual's interpretation could be false—or it could be accurate. Perhaps the term insight should be reserved for the accurate. Assuming that insight should be reserved to define the accurate, the question becomes is insight desirable, if, for example, the person *is* inferior? In such cases perhaps it would be better if the person were encouraged to formulate a more idealized approach. A further question involves the stage in an individual's development at which he can accept self-insight; the individual needs a structure of security and of "self-coping" behavior. Insight could be psychologically destructive before a certain point.

Self-insight is sometimes defined as that which is in accord with the view of oneself that the majority of outsiders have—an attributed identity and, in effect, a form of reality-testing situation; but this definition is not entirely satisfying. A better definition of self-insight is that condition when the person understands himself and his motives entirely apart from the reactions of others. Self-insight is a personal matter existing within the individual as a product of his own cognitive-affective processes. Ultimate reality is the person's own perception, not someone else's.

Chapter 13

Research Entry to the Study of Self-Process

Research and Self-Theory

A scientific theory is valuable only if it is heuristic and so formulated that it is susceptible to refutation or corroboration by rigorously designed research. A scientist wishing to put forward a comprehensive theory constructs systems of hypotheses based upon his postulates and tests them by observation, experiment, and other available methods. Such testing is a lengthy process often impeded by problems of methodology and instrumentation. The theorist's problem is complicated if the proposed theory deals with apparently unobservable inferred processes and states so that research must be accomplished by indirect means. If the theory does deal with unobservables the theorist's first task is to find a point of entry for preliminary testing of inferences and predictions. The collection of descriptive data is frequently a necessary initial step preceding controlled experimentation.[1] The advisability of looking and listening as a preliminary step

---

[1] Description is a basis for experimentation, but experimentation frequently indicates the need for further description before additional experimentation can be accomplished. The situation is: description → experimentation → description → experimentation. Of course, experimentation is not the only method of science. Horrocks (1964) notes four methods of science: experimentation, measurement, observation, and case history.

necessary for an understanding of what can be researched or what is happening before stating "why" or "if-then" has been made explicit by Polanyi (1958), Inhelder and Piaget (1958), Freud (1904), Thomas and Znaniecki (1918), Keniston (1968), and James (1890).[2]

Theory-based research on self presents a number of difficulties. Self-process is essentially internal to the organism and accessible to an observer only indirectly in those aspects of external behavior which may be hypothesized to be manifestations of self-process. From such observed behaviors inferences about the nature of the underlying internal processes have to be tested. The writers have stressed their theoretical assumptions of the importance of role behavior as an expression of self. It is their opinion that role behavior provides the point of entry for basic research on self-process and its resulting self-conceptualizations. From such role behavior research, given appropriate methodology and instrumentation, preliminary tests of a theory of self may be made that could lead to the formulation of further research even closer to the organism's internal behavior. Thus, while role behavior serves as an entry point, research on self eventually must move beyond role behavior. Further comprehensive research on self will have to consider all of the elements of self-process, including cognition, affect, drives and needs, values, attribution of meaning, learning, retrieval, and social interaction.

Purpose of Initial Research Reported

The initial research for testing the theoretical system proposed in the preceding chapters of this volume was designed to utilize a small number of individuals and, by means of semi-structured sequential in-depth interviews, to gain as many insights as possible into their processes of self-development as determined by identities and their manifestation in role behaviors. The purpose of the interviews was, to

[2] James wrote, "Self . . . seems to be basic for all human beings, and it is strange for a science so to construe its domain of interest that fundamental and universal observations are ruled out of bounds. . . . Moreover it is a realm of observation with which we are concerned in considering the problems of self."

a limited extent, to gain: (a) evidence to lend credibility to assumptions upon which the theory is based, (b) additional evidence to elaborate primary postulates, (c) further suggestions for variables important to the process of self-development, (d) evidence casting doubt upon some of the proposed assumptions of self in roles, and (e) an indication of possibilities for next research steps. In short, the research presented in this chapter was designed to provide data from which inductive and deductive inferences can be made relating to both self-process and role behaviors. The research is an attempt to discover whether researchable variables do exist and thus is *a priori* to defining the variables and controls necessary for next research steps.

The research methods described fail to meet certain objective criteria for data gathering in the behavioral sciences. The design precludes the use of ordinary controls, the setting of dependent and independent variables, and elimination of subjective biases. A premise underlying the selection of the design used, however, is that typical research methods, although quantifiable and statistically valuable, would not enable the achievement of the objectives of the preliminary study.

Sample

The sample consisted of nine white males, eight of whom were in advanced formal educational training for either professional or academic careers. One of the subjects, selected as a "ballast" member of the sample, had dropped out of school in the tenth grade but eventually attained a high school equivalency diploma while in military service. This sample cannot be taken as representative of any population nor can it be a basis for statistical analysis. Averaging of sample response frequencies would serve little purpose and would create an illusion of homogeneity of variance. The selection of an "older" group of young adults was based on the assumption that people in transition stages between, or in anticipation of, change in roles or in concepts of self offer the most profitable interviews. As Anna Freud (1958) has stated, adolescents are difficult subjects for self-analysis, a fact which would defeat the demands of the present methodology.

These participants were willing, capable, and interested individuals. They were as different in their background experiences as any eclectic group of humans, yet they were assumed to possess similarities.

Interviews

Information from the respondents was gained by a semi-structured interview technique.[3] As White (1952) contends "Any attempt to study other people must rely heavily on interviews. There can be no other adequate substitute for the obvious procedure of asking the subject to tell all that he can about himself and his environment."

The semi-structured interview format used is a composite of the following approaches: (a) Adlerian historical data gathering technique, (b) Wolberg's (1954) technique for case study, (c) a modification of White's (1952) method of interview and Keniston's (1968) co-researcher technique, (d) a modified autobiography as proposed by Thomas and Znaniecki (1918), and (e) specific "lead" items relating to self-concepts, behavior, roles, values, goals, and interpersonal relationships.[4] This format culled information concerning family, perceived inter-relationships of family and significant others with respect to the interviewee, discipline, ideals, early memories, fantasies, school and social relationships, interests, problems, fears, attitudes and beliefs, value formations, specific events, situations and behavioral responses, aspirations and goals of present and future, anticipations of contextual and social change, perceptions of continuity or discontinuity in expectations of self, and present role status and probability of role occurrences. The natural progression of conversation was the impetus for the questions generated by the interviewer. The interviewer was guided by item contents although pertinent items were directly asked by participants whenever it was deemed necessary.

---

[3] The interview format may be found in Appendix A.

[4] The combination of these methods enabled the interviewee to free associate and respond to direct questions of events and experiences of past, present, and future conditions. The interviewee's comments focused on both reality probabilities and on non-reality possibility bases.

Procedure

The data presented in this chapter are incidents selected as illustrations. Each session of the interviews lasted a maximum of two hours for a maximum of three sessions, spaced approximately one week to ten days apart. The interviews were held privately at the convenience of the interviewee, usually in the evening. The conversations were tape recorded on two hour cassettes.

Interviewees were permitted to free associate but were somewhat structured in their thoughts by responding to "lead" questions that acted as stimuli for possible digressions. At times the responses were quite elaborate and tangential to the purposes of the investigation. However, the informal nature of the interview permitted a comfortable conversational atmosphere. Further, the interviewees were not sure what the questioner was "looking for" in their responses (this was mentioned by them in their post interview discussions) and, as a result, the content of their responses, as well as the quality of information they divulged, tended to be less biased and less restrictive than would otherwise have been the case.

Subjects' voluntary involvement in this research was a prime prerequisite for their inclusion in the sample. No compensation was offered and the subjects were neither institutionalized nor in therapy. Only those young adults who were willing, were non-threatened by the prospects of personal disclosure, and were intrigued by participating in a study of themselves were interviewed. The participants were informed that they were co-researchers (as Keniston suggests) and experimental subjects (as White contends) and by relating their thoughts and behaviors in perspective to their interpretations of context and self, they would provide substantiation or refutation or suggest alternative hypotheses for an empirical study of "self."

A minimum of interviewees' comments will be presented for illustrative purposes in the sections of this chapter which follow to provide information concerning: (a) the construction of concepts of self as identity concepts, (b) saliency or importance of substantiated identity concepts, (c) continuity

or discontinuity of self-meaning over time, (d) broader interpretations of self across situations, (e) types of role behaviors
evidenced, (f) subjective interpretations by respondent of
factors influencing manifestations of self through roles,
(g) effects of values on self-exemplifications, (h) implications
for locus of control behavior, (i) effects of awareness of reality
or non-reality on identity concepts, and (j) consistency or
inconsistency in behavior. The first four items (a-d) focus
on presentation of comments relating to self as process; the
remaining six (e-j) focus on self manifested in role behavior.

Development of Identity Concepts

An attempt was made to discern how subjects cognitively
conceptualize self-references, assuming that identity concepts
could be obtained from interviews by relating perceived
similarities, differences, and similar or opposite relationships
to specific others or role representatives. The first method
employed was to ask the subjects to describe someone who
was *most like* them. Illustrative of comparisons made are the
following:

> (Name) had similar feelings to me, and same aspirations
> and same positions, work, . . . we went all through school
> together . . . have a shared destiny as far as what we'd like
> to do . . . he is kind, trustworthy, honest. . . . (later he
> defines himself as) kind, considerate, honest, personal in-
> tegrity, trustworthy.
>
> My wife . . . her belief in higher values of middle class
> . . . honest. Her belief in the sacredness of marriage, and the
> purity with which it should be upheld, and her high goals as
> far as her relations to humanity and fellow man.

One interviewee described himself as avoiding conflict but
related that his younger sister would fight (beat up his tor-
mentors). He said, "I never fought with anybody. I tended to
compromise, avoid conflict . . . also a characteristic of my
mother."

The next method used asked the interviewees to describe
someone who was *most different* from themselves. The following comments refer to those people who were perceived as
most different from the subject. By elaboration, the inter-

viewees identify identity concepts not perceived in their exemplar that they hypothesized for themselves. Some examples:

> In many ways my brother is like me but very different. He is what I'd be like if I didn't go to college . . . I'm aware of his feelings, his values and politics. He can't see my point although I could see his . . . (he describes brother, and father in a family composite statement) . . . But I think to a large extent I'm very opposite, like in religion . . . it's meaningless to me and ah, this, you know, you can't say anything about your country, you know, if you say anything wrong . . . He has no room for improvement (He continues differentiating self from father). My father was very critical and harsh, maybe that's why in certain areas I never got any feeling of confidence. I definitely feel that, on the other hand, trying to be sincere and genuine and not put on a big show I got from him . . . but I tend to think differently, more logically and rationally, in terms of alternatives, for instance, politics, if they don't like him (a politician) they won't listen to him . . . you can't discuss things . . . raise voices . . . You can see blood pressures rising.

Other comments referred to specific people as different. These comments were usually the most detailed. Within the comments a reference to similarities as well as differences of the exemplar to the interviewee was observed. Having a base for reference made constructing comparisons easy. Later comments show that meaningful reference points for conceptualization are necessary to construct a concept. Without categorization criteria, the person cognitively restructures and reorganizes data until he can construct a concept.

Illustrations of the thinking process involved are derived from subjects' descriptions of areas of difference between self and another individual perceived as important. One interviewee who neither wanted nor perceived himself to be an authoritative person saw his father as "always playing the role of king, the authority." Another interviewee referring to an uncle as different in important ways that conflict with his standards said,

> He is more independent than I am and probably more involved in bettering and improving his own career at what

I consider to be the expense of some, what are to me, more personal relationships.

This same subject later describes two friends as both like him and different in certain respects.

> They both have a very good sense of humor—sharp wit. They enjoy being together, both of them need other people and they enjoy their work, they enjoy their students—just like people—like to be around people . . . I'm older and a little more mature, I'm not as athletic, I'm a little bit different personality in the sense that I am a little more stable, a little more mature. Of course this may be a function of age.

Another respondent attempting to compare himself to another person related,

> I'm most like Dad . . . I guess I am . . . I picked up his sense of humor. At times I'm tense, but I have this paradox, too, looseness. I have a tolerance of values . . . but area of humor comes closest. Strangely enough sometimes at home we tell jokes, bad puns. I was closest to Mother. She would talk out what Dad was supposed to have done. There would be scenes, we children didn't know how to react to it. Dad was somewhat at a distance . . . I had empathy with him, sympathy with her . . . set the emotional tone of my later life . . . atuned with hers, I'm very sensitive.

The third method used to arrive at conceptualizations pertaining to self required the respondents to relate and describe someone they knew who fit certain descriptive terms (or concepts). The respondents were usually capable of describing a personification of a given concept when they set the standards or criteria for defining the concept. For instance, they were asked, "Who do you know that is ———?" After describing the concept in terms of attributes of an exemplar, the interviewees were asked to compare themselves. In this manner, each interviewee cognitively formulated the standards for a concept. The interviewee stated how he perceived himself in terms of attributes or instances of a concept (Glaser, 1968) represented by the exemplar. This method permitted each interviewee to idiographically rate himself using self-criteria established for polar points for the extent or quality of difference each respondent perceived, i.e., "I'm like that," "I'm not like that." This type of analysis enabled each subject to locate himself with reference to an exemplar by constructing an anchorage or point of origin against which he could compare himself.

Such a comparison enabled a breakdown of a larger concept (e.g., idealist, moody) which is the organization of integrated attributes perceived as defining a specific human stimuli—in this case the exemplar. The identity concepts formed by the interviewee were assumed to be the result of differentiating and reintegrating the attributes of the exemplar and reclassifying these attributes into a concept that symbolized and individuated the interviewee. In building comparisons between self and exemplar the subjects were capable of differentiating between self and exemplar and divulged a multitude of identity concepts. With the ability to cognitively conceptualize self-references the interviewees were capable of postulating identity concepts they perceived as specific or as unique self-references.

The following are excerpts of comments serving to describe how the interviewees constructed their concepts of self with reference to a given concept by contrasting themselves to an exemplar. The first example refers to the concept of "handsome" or "good-looking."

> (Name) is probably one of the nicest looking guys I know. He's not tall and he's not real dark but he is attractively slender and yet quite athletic. . . . He doesn't wear his hair real long but medium long and it looks nice, and he's got a lot of hair which is attractive to me since that's one of my few good features. . . . However, I'm decidedly inferior to him in looks and in body formation and facial expression and probably speed and agility of movement.[5]

Attempting to describe "popular," this interviewee interpreted the concept by combining the attributes of a few persons to formulate his exemplar. He said:

> I guess I don't think of any particular person, I kind of think of a composite of two or three of the kids I went to school with who summed it up for me, at least what it meant to be popular . . . I guess my definition of popularity is someone who is socially attractive and socially effective. I, in

[5] The interviewee is described by the investigator as approximately six feet, with dark hair, and slender build.

high school for instance was kind of medium in both areas. I guess I felt like that at the time . . . It may have been a rationalization, and I'm not sure it's true but I felt like at the time, that probably negative prohibitions of my family kept me from being as socially attractive as I might have been if I had been freer to conform to the normal behavior of my peer group at the time. As far as social effectiveness is concerned, I was a good student. I was in the band and some of the choral groups and so I was fairly effective socially in a sense. Although not . . . well here again, medium in athletics, fair . . . made the first team usually in baseball but not in any other sports, and a kind of medium actually in both areas, social effectiveness and social attractiveness.

An examination of this comment reveals the subject is capable not only of defining and describing self with the exemplars but also of rating himself on some cognitively constructed continuum.

Other subjects conceptualized identities by the same method. In response to the term "idealistic" one subject said:

(Name) he's a member of (Clergy). He spends lots of time in thoughts. He sets up his life in idealistic goals . . . I think at one time I had invested a lot of my time being idealistic. Now I'm 60 per cent skeptical and 40 per cent romantic. I see all possibilities. I spent blocks of time in romantic and idealistic thinking . . . At one time I entered (profession) as a means of salvation.

However, sometimes some of the subjects were unable to define concepts in terms of standards of self. Because they did not have a standard which they had previously developed, they had difficulty perceiving an exemplar for that concept. For instance, a subject was asked, "Whom do you consider to be the most masculine person you know?," he responded:

Anybody? I got to give that some serious thought in terms of my interpretations of stereotype . . . I don't think, hmm, . . . particular masculine, eh, . . . is one who reeks of sinew and, acts in tough masculine ways. That's a caricature of it. To me, masculine is in terms of responsiveness to others. Ah, a popular singer? To me, its unmasculine to be hung up on masculine . . . People I know? . . . They enhance . . .funny, I jump from one stereotype to another. I would think the ideal man is one who exhibits most of traits of a stereotype, independent, assertive, self-sufficient to some extent, but not too much and is responsive to other people's needs and wants, other people's feelings and also has sensitivity and awareness, and in certain aspects, gentleman. Lots come close, lots of fellows. Maybe I'm building an image of myself? It's not too far, not too dissonant. I'm not unmasculine . . . Yes, in terms of my definition, the things I value, I fit it, yes.

To summarize, these excerpts illustrate the assumption that identity concepts are formulated by the individual as cognitive constructions or representations of himself. When the interviewer presented any concept, the subject was able to interpret the concept in terms that related to him. They cognitively reconstructed instances or attributes observable in others that were self-references. These "instances" were reclassified by reassessment and provided a basis for an identity concept from the concept offered by the interviewer. This method was useful even when the concept was not originally perceived as applicable to self, because the interpretation of the concept permitted the interviewee to think through all the attributes that might be included within the concept. By distinguishing the attributes of the concept, the subject could then react to each attribute as a perception or representation of himself.

Specific Role Representatives in Identity Concept Formation

The subjects also were asked to describe someone they perceived as outstanding. After describing that individual they were asked to compare themselves to that person. Comments were related to specific people and the role in society they (the role exemplar) represented. The role representative was described as a status or position figure in society, such as a father, professor, economist, politician, or friend. These "outstanding" persons or role representatives were usually persons who were currently important to the respondee and were perceived as someone they fantasized as similar to themselves, or someone they would "like to be like," or to emulate in the near future. The respondee attributed to this person those concepts of self he perceived or hypothesized as highly desirable in himself. But in most cases these identity concepts were cognitions exemplified only in role figmenting behavior.

> He's a funny guy. You can't figure him out. But I consider him an outstanding guy. He can function well in any field. He's a real intellectual, in all areas. I'd like to think some day I'll know art like him . . . Sometimes he's kind of authoritarian . . . I'm not up there but I'm adequate . . . it'll depend upon discipline. I think of myself that way, as trying to be understanding and open minded. . . . I try to consider how others feel.
>
> An outstanding person? Senator (Name). He was a publisher of a newspaper, fine family, pretty sharp, lots of financial backing, a very giving person, strong, almost inflexible, gentle, great understanding, politically a philosopher. But, I'm no comparison, even now I don't have the opportunity to do what he did.

The identity concepts this subject perceived as important to himself at various points in his interview were: a friendly person, a giver not a taker, gentle, loves his family, thoughtful, wants to be successful and make "tons of money," a senator or some type of politician, a maker of speeches, remembered as Boss (his name) by others. He also described himself as flexible but felt others denied this quality in him.

Another interviewee gave this account of an outstanding person.

> I've already mentioned (Name) the things he did, as a social scientist and as the person who is concerned with the things that make things really go . . . with clarity. He's to me an outstanding person and here (designating a university) in his field, he's interested in students and encourages us to think, for that I think he's outstanding. It'd be nice to see I was a "budding" him. I don't have nearly the grasp of things . . . and I look to him as some sort of a guide. In some ways his competence is something I admire and I'd like to have. (*Emphasis is the authors'.*)
>
> Again his interest and I share it with him . . . getting at essentials of something, he doesn't waste a lot of time—time efficiency is a thing I value.

The few comments presented above reveal that these subjects perceived in others qualities that they desired or hypothesized for themselves at future dates.

Saliency or Importance of Substantiated Identity Concepts

Many of the concepts of self (identities) mentioned by the interviewees and substantiated by others, were discerned by two methods. The first analysis focused on the substantiation gained by feedback from others who were perceived as significant or important to the subject. Briefly stated, the comments were:

> I'm less moody to other people . . . and I'm more moody at home. My wife commented about this, says I'm a different person around other people than I am at home.
>
> I'm not demanding at all. It's hard to point it out on a continuum but I consider myself flexible. My wife says I'm not, that I have a way of getting what I want by plotting and planning. That may be true, but, . . . I'm probably less flexible in reality than I think I am . . . And I think I do (have a temper) but I'd say it's controlled. I fight this. I'd be so happy to tell people what I think, but I know it isn't appreciated. The more education I get, the higher you go in the academic world, the least they expect it . . . and you lose academic points. It's not a good idea. But I have a few friends I can blow steam off with . . . I also have a tendency to dominate conversations. That's one of my weaknesses even to the point of sidetracking conversations other people are interested in and I'm not. My wife brings this to my attention now and then and I think she's probably correct. I'm a little bit sarcastic, too.

The second method of seeking the factors that produced saliency of substantiated concepts focused on situational factors. In this last illustration the respondent mentioned factors in situations or events that modified his behavior. He stressed the restrictions emanating from expectations of a professional nature that prevented him from "being himself," that is, manifesting himself in role behavior.

Substantiated identity concepts were cognitions modified by affective feedback. Interviewees responded to the question that attempted to cull information concerning their most important perceptions of self. One said simply, "I'm like ————, conservative . . ." but modified that reference with, "My own thoughts are not with the mass or with those called conservatives." He realized another important identity concept and relates, "You know, humor is a strong element, and it runs all through my friendships. If there is no humor, there's no friends. I hadn't thought about it, but it's an important element."

Incidents were related that show a change in salience of previously important identity concepts. The writers interpret this change as lending credibility to the premise that identity concepts are capable of change. They are flexible, reintegratable concepts reorganized to give new meanings of self.

> My most important concepts? I guess being a friendly, loving person . . . to be a giver, not a taker. Being a Christian at one time was number one, but not this time, that's not number one. But, I think I'm a damn nice guy.
>
> As a youngster, I always wanted to be in the service. I joined the ROTC. Now I'm totally against rank. Now if you gave me admiral, I'd tell you to shove it. But all my themes in high school . . . Commie threat . . . ——— ———— sun rose and set on him. All my brothers were in the service. I wanted to be in too. Besides they were in Greece and Rome, look at all the places you go and do and see in the service. Physical problem, I overcame, but eventually I was rejected . . . maybe a reaction formation?

This incident depicted a cognitive-affective reorganization of self-interpretations because of the lack of manifestation of identity concepts that had previously been role taken and role figmented many times during his youth. He stated that as a youth he always played soldier with toy guns (not sticks) and knapsacks, and imagined himself in the service in his favorite fantasies. When he was an ROTC candidate, he was able to manifest his hypothesized identities in role taking behavior by assuming a soldier role. Eventually, however, situational and physical factors prevented the substantiation of that identity concept in his identity assemblage. The assemblage is a hypothetical construct representing cognitive structuring of important identities that give a meaning or interpretation of self at any particular time and across situations.

Continuity of Self: Constancy of Percepts

Concepts of self originating from somatic references showed interesting constancies. Self-interpetation derived from concepts of somatic reference showed a constancy of self-perceptions despite physical changes. The constancy of concepts of self may have been the result of two conditions. The first condition is the influence of interpreting prior identity concepts into current self-meanings, a reassociation or reintegration process. A second condition for constant manifestation of certain identity concepts is that somatic identity concepts are *important* concepts and salient features of meaning, persisting over time. These concepts of somatic identities are heavily affect-modified cognitions and appear to be interrelated with other conceptualizations regarding athletic ability, illness or healthiness percepts, height, weight, strength and physical prowess. The following excerpts are presented to lend credence to both of the postulated influencing factors.

> As far as looks I've always had an inferiority complex. I always thought I was the ugliest. I was pretty ugly, skin and bones, stature-concave chest, big hole in chest, lordosis, curvature of the spine, rounded shoulders. I'd say pretty ugly. I was always a little bit smaller, to me it seemed so. Even though others were smaller, wiry types I just wasn't. Now since I got married, I'd gotten up to be a big slob, 180, but I'm down now at 160. I wear clothes to hide my defects. I go swimming and it doesn't bother me now. I don't idolize body men, but I don't compete with them. I don't mind, really mind, competing with a popular idol type because I think I got more to offer in certain ways. My looks are still below average, below par, I got a big beak, don't consider myself handsome . . . I would make an effort to keep my weight down, you know, man my age, heart—everything you read . . . I am also dress conscious. I don't want to look sloppy, fashionable at the time . . . I shave to go out. Shop more than the average guy and I can't stand body odor.

Or,

> I was a little kid, a scrawny kid, and I can't think of anything distinctive. I was a funny looking kid, I always had my arm in a cast. Now I'm not as scrawny. I see myself as being small and wish I was bigger. I admire bigger people, bigger men, anyhow. Now I don't think I'm funny looking. I'm at least average as far as looks are concerned. I haven't had any girls attack me (laughs). I would like to think I was taller. I would loved to have played football. I don't think of myself as wanting to be someone else (now).

One interviewee stressed his identity concepts of "good-looking" by the feedback he had received. He summed up his conceptualization of self in the following comment, "In general, I think I'm goodlooking. The only way you can tell, is you get feedback from people. My wife thinks I am goodlooking, . . . in height, and strength."

In order to determine whether there was continuity of self over time the questions focused on the description of themselves as youth and on the comparison of the youthful meanings of self to their present definitions of self. As youths, these subjects perceived important identity concepts that had been resubstantiated many times in many roles throughout their experiences. One subject related a manifestation of an identity concept that became pervasive through most of his percepts of self.

> My mother is mentally ill . . . has been committed to several institutions five years ago. In retrospect it was ongoing as long as I can remember. I thought it was marital troubles, fights. I can remember accusations . . . aware of it to the extent I was quite involved. I envisioned myself as a peacemaker. I was involved in keeping peace between Mother and Dad. I intervened. From my view, my role was as peacemaker. (*Underlines by the writers.*)

At a later point in the interview sessions, he summarized his "overall or general" self description. He stated ". . . *involvement* in interaction with Mother and Dad made me what I am—a peacemaker . . . forced me to see two points of view in any confrontation and makes me ask what the heck is going on." The writers have emphasized certain phrases in the above comments. These words indicate that the individual is role taking and not role playing in roles as in intervener or peacemaker. It would seem from his commentary that he originally *figmented* himself as a peacemaker ("I envisioned myself" . . .) but, at some point he *manifested* this identity concept into his role of "son." His role taking behavior was a manifestation of the identity concept of peacemaker. His statement "I was quite *involved*" is one indication of self manifested in role behavior (or role taking behavior).

One interviewee went into great depth to explain how he

gained "specialness" in his self-meaning or individuation of self from others. An abbreviated version of his comments:

> I wanted to strive to be special, to be valued, not to be average or ordinary . . . to your peer groups you are just a (professional) so I was going to specialize. The trouble is each time you get another peer group I found myself relating to it and saying, "I don't see myself as special," and in fact I didn't get that feedback from them. It surprised me. I was just everyday with my peer group. (Now) I'm better, different and have something special to offer so that when I look for a job I'll have this on everybody. I'm different and it's difficult to define a peer group now. No one in the rest of the country has this like me, so maybe that makes me comfortable. (Earlier he commented) I probably want to be the best . . . competitive . . . I see myself as doing better than the next guy although I tend to compete with specific individuals . . . Mother would say I wanted to be the best.

It was not a difficult task for these respondents to comment on the continuity of self-meaning over time and across situations. They apparently focused on certain cognitions that are continuously substantiated by their manifestation in reality situations. Some interpretations of self were generalized and not confined to specific situations. Interpretations of self were either simply phrased or elaborated with many qualifying conceptualizations. Two comments are presented to show how each individual has defined himself.

> I consider myself moody. Sometimes I'm up and sometimes I'm down for no apparent reason. At times I'm listening to music and I don't want to share it . . . get depressed. I consider myself not particularly socially outgoing, fairly introverted . . . I enjoy being by myself especially in summer.
>
> I'll describe myself as lovable, honest, with personal integrity, capable of understanding others and empathetic and sympathetic with some problems they might have, and capable of being obstinate. I make mistakes in relating to others. But I set up a system with myself by which I become aware of these . . . I have a capability for development. I am limited in the intellectual realm. I don't have any image of being a brilliant scholar but I can contribute. I dislike the slowness with which I move, and I don't

> formulate goals in some future . . . If I was more sure of
> myself . . . I'm a plodder in some respects, and wish I
> were quicker . . . I tend to be contemplative.

At a later session, the speaker of the first quotation said, "My basic personality—no major changes. I was quiet, somewhat inhibited and there wouldn't be many kids at all I was close to." Now he sees himself as "a quiet, shy guy, I like being with a few people, . . . but less shy."

However, one subject was faced with a problem in attempting to respond to the question directed toward description of an overall or general self that was not time-event confined. He said succinctly, "One me is a very difficult thing to pin down. There are too many parts . . . I keep talking about my goal as getting all my parts together." Since it is beyond the scope of this research to probe into the reasons for any comment made by the subjects, it can only be speculated that the comments of the last respondent may have resulted from the broad range of identity conceptualizations that were formulated by him as a result of the methods used in the interview.

Self and Role Behavior

Role behaviors were described as observable and unobservable behavioral manifestations of self, and as observable behavioral responses perceived appropriate for situational demands. Conditional factors were assumed to determine the form of role behavior manifested by the individual.

Attempts were made during the interview to determine:

1 how individuals cognitively interpret situations.
2 what are the stimuli to which they knowingly react.
3 how they expect themselves to be, that is, whether self involved or performing an action.
4 whether the anti-identities are cognitive phenomena, by reference to those concepts of self expected of them that they do not hypothesize of themselves at that moment in that situation.
5 if there was a motivational effect or locus of control for role assumption.
6 if there was an awareness of reality or non-reality basis for identity concept exemplification.

7   whether factors, external to their control, limit, define or modify performance in roles.

8   whether intrinsic factors limit, define and restrict performance in roles.

During the interviews the subjects mentioned the following qualifying conditions when asked how they behave in *specific* social, educational, personal, or occupational interactive situations. The situations were described as role specific. A partial listing of their comments is presented to identify a few of the factors which were consciously attended to or acknowledged by the interviewees as affecting their manifestations of identity concepts.

1   really depends on the situation

2   depends on how he reacts to me . . . it's that—I react

3   but here, I'm supposed to take the initiative

4   at a party . . . I hesitate . . . I tap the situation

5   In a group . . . I was the only student . . . I think I spent all my time sizing up what *they're going* to be like.

6   I size up the situation . . . what kind . . . what level . . . who's there.

7   got to be careful about what you wear, not to be too swaggy . . . what you say

8   I'd be very choosy about the areas we'd talk about.

9   I'd feel inhibited, worried about *faux pas*.

10   I'd have a more sexual frame of reference (with girls) than I do in church.

11   It depends on the size of the class, professor, who's in it.

12   I'm afraid to be me, to be completely free because of personalities.

13   certain situations call for certain things from you

14   have to do things that are socially acceptable—something I don't like to do but I do it

15   to get to where I want . . . I have to do a lot of ————— . . . have to play and kiss a lot of —————

16   the restrictions and responsibilities on me . . .

17   If someone was watching me, I *might* do it (under pressure from performance demands).

18   I do it matter of factly and I'd have no interest.
19   I can't always be honest . . . it's the "politic" thing
      to do.
20   It's the fact you got to do it, but I'll learn to cope and
      do it.
21   the male role dictates males don't cry
22   I feel compelled to have to say it's great when it's
      adequate.
23   They were expecting me to behave differently.
24   groups have an inhibitory effect in putting myself
      across
25   with authoritarians . . . I'm not about to be myself
26   To some extent I mask or hide my identity in certain
      situations.

Role Taking and Role Playing Behaviors

The comments reveal a consciousness or awareness by the individuals of factors that influenced their manifestation of identity concepts through role behavior. Many of the requirements mentioned were situational or imposed by the demands of social interaction. In some of the interview discussions the respondents found it difficult to state how they perceived themselves, or wanted to present themselves in specific roles because their behavior in these roles depended upon many factors. The way they perceived a role was largely determined by their self-conceptions, situational cues, their values, and the benefits they perceived from the role in terms of both their self needs and others' expectations. Many subjects could describe how they hypothesized they might act and how they *did* act in certain roles by estimating what effects they would or did have on the situation and what the situational requirements they anticipated might be.

One interviewee described how he perceived himself and his behavior in a friend role:

> It depends on how he reacts to me. On the whole it's that, I react. I'm not gregarious. I don't usually take initiative, but here I'm supposed to take initiative, but socially, I don't start. That's not me.

The subject refers to both role playing demands and his reaction to the imposed anti-identity, "That's not me."

In a professional role another subject described what transpired when he was required to perform a role he had not previously had the opportunity to assume or through which he could not confidently substantiate identity concepts.

> They're expecting me to behave differently . . . since I have been a student for eleven years when I went down there I should be saying Dr. So and So with a great deal of respect. Instead I found myself saying, "Yes, Ted," this and other, and being uncomfortable with it. But I felt I was expected to be considered a peer, and should behave that way . . . To some extent, I'm not sure of what's appropriate or inappropriate for I haven't played that particular role for very long or had much experience . . . At the time I responded to a situation . . . The next time, I think I'll approach it a little differently.

Another subject described an incident of conflicting roles.

> I can't stand to sit around and nod to people. I do it sometimes because . . . one of the criticisms I get is I'm too aggressive. For instance, (at work) I disagreed with some of her interpretations. The role that was reinforced was to "play student" and I don't like to play student . . . I don't like to be dependent. At times, uh, I like to be dependent.

It appears from this comment that the subject is required to role play a "student role" while he reacts strongly to the demands placed upon him by assuming the role—that of being "dependent." This concept "dependency" was an anti-identity that he was expected to manifest as a self-percept, as appropriate for the role performance. In this situation the conflict of role playing an anti-identity that was at variance with his self-conceptualizations resulted in defense mechanisms. Another incident reported by an interviewee who attempted to role take an identity concept for reality testing through a student role resulted in his retreating or "disengaging" his self from the role performance.

> I suppose I take the role of a provocateur. I like to express myself and my ideas. But it depends upon the instructor. I sometimes play "nice student" if I feel it

> wasn't my place in his classroom. I'm conscious of my role,
> sometimes I trip up. I'm more and more aware. I expect
> myself to enter into discussions. I won't sit back and let the
> class go by without saying two words. But larger groups
> have an inhibitory effect in putting myself across to others.
> I start frank, start speaking . . . jovial . . . see if they
> match up my sense of humor with theirs and if I get a cool
> reaction, I disengage, I back out.

When the subject attempted to reality test an identity concept through role taking behavior, the feedback he received
was encoded as modifying cognitive concepts of self. To alleviate cognitive dissonance caused by a discrepancy between
anticipation of acceptance and feedback of the manifestation
of his hypothesized identity in a reality situation he "dis-
engages" or withdraws from the situation the identity he
postulated for himself. Further information was not available about what he did in the situation after he had with-
drawn or had divested his self from exemplification in that
role.

This excerpt also presents a self-reflexiveness factor ("I expect myself . . ."). The interaction is reflected or directed
back onto his hypothesized identity concept and becomes a
self-reflexive condition of role taking. This condition is the
result of processing feedback from others in a social interaction onto self. Since this individual became "disengaged" and
withdrew his identity concept from the role, it is assumed that
non-acceptance by others was cognitively encoded and had
affect-modified the conceptualization of self.

Many incidents related by the subjects were attempts to
respond to their perceptions of others' acceptance or non-
substantiation of their exemplification of self in role taking
behavior.

> (as a teacher) I was shy, students have misperceptions.
> They think I'm dogmatic, authoritarian . . . (He does not
> perceive himself as an authoritarian figure, just shy, quiet,
> capable of mutual understanding, non-dogmatic).
> I think others think I'm ambitious.
> Sometimes I get the feeling from peers around here, they
> think I know more than I normally do.
> They think I'm smarter, understanding, attending, but

> I'm capable of disappointing others because I try to convey good, kind and understanding and don't always act that way.
>
> Brashness—my wife says I talk fiercely and say things I don't mean, and this offends people. I've toned down. I don't feel I want to be brash.
>
> People think I'm much more Christ-centered than I think I am. Some of my friends doubt my sincerity about being one or the other. That's the way they see me and I don't.

One subject described how he perceived himself and how he perceived others responding to him. The first part of his comments refer to his role taking and role figmenting behaviors.

> (as a student) They used to call me Boss (Name). We ran the political machine that ran the student body. (His role figmenting was to be a senator or political figure, making speeches, and tons of money.)
>
> (at work) Oh, I played the part . . . I was the darling, the junior executive on his way up. I sought out the key men in the department much to the disgust of my co-workers . . . Then I got into the insurance business—there's a lot of acting as a salesman. You just don't go out in a dumpy mood and sell. You got to be happy, interested in people, especially selling.

The latter part of his comments suggests that in order to achieve his aspirations he had to role play, adhering to performances or behavioral responses perceived as obligatory for achieving the rewards he desired. A corollary of role playing (see Chapter 10) states that the locus of control for role playing behavior is extrinsic to the individual. An individual responds to the reinforcements in external conditions for the rewards he seeks. In this case the interviewee states he role plays the "up and coming junior executive" effectively with anticipation that the rewards he seeks will be granted. According to Homan's (1958) economic exchange principles (a social-balance theory), accruable benefits are measured in amount of expenditures. In this case the expenditure was in effective, convincing performance and not in investment of concepts of self.

Another individual discussed the effects of responding to

contextual demands which were at times variant with his concepts of self. He stated:

> I'm the middle of the road type, between my values and integrity, and my expectations and views of what they expect. I will cater to their expectations if I think they are at all reasonable, but if it violates too much what are some of the things I believe in, I rationalize or get out of the situation.

This individual apparently has been able to cognitively alleviate the dissonance he receives from assuming an anti-identity. However, he is restricted from accepting anti-identities that violate his values. In order to remove "cognitive strain" or "cognitive dissonance," he either reorganizes his cognitions to accept a new interpretation of the anti-identity, or, if that cannot be or is not accomplished, he withdraws himself from the role by no longer participating in the situation or in the social act.

Situational Cues for Self-Manifestation in Roles

If situations were perceived as new, strange, or threatening, the subjects usually performed a role by role-playing behaviors. Many situations or sequences of behavior that emitted role-playing behavior were difficult to elicit from the respondents because they did not wish to convey the impression of falseness or acting. However, to some subjects role responses that satisfied situational requirements were considered natural behavioral reactions. To others, the awareness of threat, or potential threat in new or strange situations, or situations in which they would not "be involved" or feigned interest was a reason for role playing. They role played in order to adjust to the behavioral requirements they perceived as an obligation of the role into which they were placed.

Some interviewees interpreted situations as "threatening" to important substantiated self-meanings and changed role-taking behaviors into role playing, or immediately role played until they felt secure in manifesting an identity concept for reality testing in a role.

> I'm sensitive and I feel comfortable being vulnerable when I think the other person is not going to hurt me for being

vulnerable. But if I think he has the power to hurt and he's going to hurt me, then I put up the swaggering "Cool Man" kind of stuff. As I told you before with new relationships sometimes, as when we talked about women . . . that the situation demanded it . . . makes me put up air of coolness.

In threatening situations . . . not benefit anything by revealing self. With an authoritarian professor, I'm not about to be myself and expose my values to that kind of person.

I put up a shell . . .

Perhaps if you're not skillful, you can give the impression of being false by being considerably different than you are. (*Note that skill is a performance criterion.*)

Role playing occurs naturally in social interactions where certain behavioral responses are required of the individual. This individual describes how his profession requires him to project a certain image of himself.

I'd like to be able to complain . . . to let my hair down like at home and act the way I feel. But I usually try to keep a stiff upper lip around people that I don't know well or that don't know me well, and have had people ask me why I was so cheerful when I wasn't really cheerful at all. I simply emulate optimism, I think, in situations where I'm not well known or do not know the people well.

In friendly situations perceived as not demanding specific behavioral responses, the subjects more readily engaged in role-taking behavior by manifesting identity concepts they hypothesized for themselves, or, for which they sought resubstantiation. These situational cues provided information about role requirements and were the type of situation in which the respondents described themselves as being "involved" or "comfortable" with themselves and others.

Role-Figmenting Behavior

The subjects, even in adult years, engaged in figmenting identities. Closely related to figmenting identities in roles were their aspirations for their self-image, especially with respect to position and status roles. Some of the figmented identities conceptualizations were consistently recurring in their fantasies. For instance:

> When I was a child I used to want to be a pilot and an aeronautical engineer. Now I still want to be a pilot but my wife opposes it and it's expensive.

Two factors prevent this identity concept from being exemplified. The first factor is his wife's opposition, and the second factor is the cost of training. Both these factors are related to reality. Since role-figmenting behavior is non-reality based, the restrictions placed upon the role assumption of being a pilot were not a deterrent in the individual's role-figmenting behavior.

Another subject describes a role-figmenting behavior he engages in simultaneously while role taking.

> Yes, some of these are fairly imaginary, like when I play athletics. I had kind of emulated (names). I'd take an imaginary stance, how they (the sports figures he emulates) handle the ball. Now, when I still play, I'd think about how they hit, serve.

Some role-figmenting behaviors are overtly manifested in play situations through which the make-believe element forms the acceptable condition for non-reality based identity concepts.

> I used to like to be in the military. I saw myself as someone in the service. As a youngster I used to play military. It had to be realistic, no sticks for guns, knapsacks, . . . (as an older child) I imagined myself in the occupations of my brothers, as army soldiers.

Role-figmenting behavior is closely related to aspirations for self in the near or not too distant future. One interviewee saw himself as a "prophet," another imagined himself as a "future pioneer," or "I perceive myself as a hero" or "embodied in people who can be powerful."

The following is an excerpt of one subject who felt that much of his satisfaction was obtained from figmenting identity concepts. When asked if he daydreamed or had fantasies, he remarked:

> All the time . . . I'm a Walter Mitty type character . . . all sorts of fun things, like, that I'm giving speeches, getting elected to Congress, and doing little more in the limelight here and there. Oh, I've probably seduced more women in

> dreams than Carter has liver pills. I've always been a day-
> dreamer. I don't understand anybody who doesn't daydream.
> Sex would be number one . . . Favorite? Oh yes, political,
> being a senator, being Ole Boss (name). But, that's a
> fantasy in this stage of life.

This interviewee was not anticipating the manifestation of his
favorite fantasy in reality. The opportunity for role taking as
a politician was not perceived as available to him.

An interesting group of responses centered on the question
of work and its meaning in terms of self as exemplified in
certain roles. Since this type of response diverges slightly
from the focus of this interview series only those comments
related to self in roles will be mentioned. One of the distinctions presented by some of the respondents was that "there is
a difference between a position and a job" or "between work
and occupation." Work was defined as "my mission in life"
whereas "job or occupation was toil." Another interviewee
elaborated and said, "my fulfillment is in work." To the question asking what either work or occupation means, this man
commented:

> That distinction was made fairly clearly to me last year,
> work and a job. I take a job as something you do to make
> money, whereas work you do out of interest, out of what
> you want to do. That is the distinction I virtually hold.
> I don't want to work at a job. Work has some sort of
> meaning; work contributes knowledge, enlightenment, self-
> importance; money isn't always a goal. I want in my work
> some sort of self-satisfaction and accomplishment and criti-
> cal acceptance by peers.

When work is defined in terms of satisfaction of self, by
substantiations of identity concepts in meaningful roles, then
work is not perceived as a job but as intrinsically meaningful
to the self-needs, as well as fulfilling society's obligations for
adult responsibility.

Results of Role Assumptions to Self

An interesting variety of responses were made when the interviewees discussed their fears. There seemed to be a range
of fearful conditions but on elaboration the locus of fear was

related to the perceptions of self. Some of the fears directly impinged upon structuring self-meanings, whereas other fears were founded upon violation of values that were criteria for self. One individual feared a loss of self-control—a fear of locus of control of his own behavior, by being vulnerable to manipulation. This is a very interesting area for study of self and, when approached in depth, could reveal highly important or salient concepts of self. These concepts are capable of producing loss of self-meaning if they are denied manifestation as identity concepts for that individual. A brief variety of "fears" is included.

> My fear of abandonment . . . my fear of insecurity . . . fear in getting the Ph.D. that I might have to sacrifice personal integrity and it'd not be worth it.
> I always became involved with one person, committed . . . I wish that I wasn't that way. Person who is less committed to a person is in control of the situation . . . Person who is involved is vulnerable to being manipulated.
> Those things that violate my values or personal integrity. I fear I'll be a "camille," a dishonest individual . . . hideous.
> As a male I'd like to keep intact physically . . . Right now though, it's fear of failure . . . this defines my life . . . fear of failure, fear of not being able to live up to someone's standards I met. Even as a child I feared not being able to accomplish what I set for myself.

The comments were focused on a fear of implied external threats that would cause a loss of self primarily through loss of control of what was important to self.

Values: Intrinsic Factor Modifying Self in Role Behavior

Values were previously defined by the writers as standards and criteria for conduct or actions, and end states or ideals and goals. In the interviews values were described by the respondents as determinants for molding interpretations of self and for the meanings derived by cognitively evaluating identity concepts manifested in socially available roles. By manifesting identity concepts in role taking behavior an individual can evaluate himself by the self-standards he has cognitively formulated.

The importance of values to structuring and maintaining a

self-meaning is shown in some of the following comments. Values are restrictive to certain responses the individual may be expected to perform.

> Value most, personal integrity, ideas I consider my own, being honest with myself. My own man, but I can be pressured to go along. Being faithful to ideas and self, what I stand for, and my goals. I don't compromise about those things. I may have to compromise with reality if I can't have them, but I suppose I'll always fight . . .
>
> Cooperation, if it didn't conflict with my values . . . (He explains a paradox he perceives.) I place some of my values within the expectations of others. It can be a delusion . . . but I don't feel coerced if I can see a relationship to later on.
>
> I don't have this charisma by which everyone I meet likes me . . . I don't go out of my framework of values to please others . . . I tend to stay within my frame of values.

When a subject described his own values he usually did so by comparing them with the values held by others. Values were individually defined and cognitively constructed. They were not an incorporation of "things" from society, but were standards and criteria that individuals ascribe to objects, people, events, and to self. To determine whether persons perceive a change in their values over time and if they felt their values were social "oughts" or personal constructed criteria the subjects responded:

> We tend to change very much from family values. Varies . . . father and mother were somewhat different. I can't get that (values) from any one person . . . it's a personal philosophy . . . train of thought, I rationalize in myself.
>
> My values have changed from what they were.

The comment reproduced below is presented as an illustration depicting the process an individual follows in applying his values. He thinks through a desired situation in terms of his values and what the effects would be. This subject cognitively evaluated (applied his criteria) what the consequences of his behavior would mean to his society and to himself.

> Well, we hit the sex thing but when you think it through as carefully as I have it's not worth it, because all you are going to do is wipe yourself out and you lose everything that's important to you. Like, in our society you just don't

do such things. And there's that feeling of getting caught. But you're always caught when you live with yourself. You'd know and that in itself is bad enough—and the fear of getting caught, you know, I'm chicken.

Summary

The interview method provided information pertaining to identity formation, structuring of meaning of self, and the relationship of self to roles.

Identity concepts formation depends upon conceptualization of self-image instances or self-representations. These representations are amenable to integration and reorganization, forming many "self or identity" type statements. The implication derived from interviews, lending credence to assumptions made by the writers, is that identity concepts are changeable and capable of differentiation and reintegration to provide concepts of self for manifestation in reality situations, or for exemplification in non-reality based contexts. These concepts can be made manifest through available social roles, but it is through the postulation of role behaviors that an investigator can begin to differentiate those performances that are intrinsically related to self and those performances that are divested of self-components. High self-risk situations, potentially threatening contexts, strange, unfamiliar or new situations, and certain demand contexts have been described as conducive to performance behavior (role playing) in which self-involvement is not a factor. Motivation, both intrinsic as shown by locus of control for investment of self-components, and extrinsic, as shown by the production of required behaviors by external reinforcements, was depicted as a factor for the form of role behavior the person assumes.

Reflexiveness was an important factor in providing information for assessing role behavior. Reflexiveness is an important construct for psychological study, applicable for self-evaluation of identity manifestation, and dependent upon the processing of others' reactions for modification of cognitively constructed identity concepts. Self-reflexiveness is postulated as a factor conditional with a reality base.

A non-self-reflexive factor results from interactive behavior. The actor performs an action, and the results of his actions, as evaluated by others, are cognitively assimilated as performance effectiveness and not reflected into self-structures.

The interview method has generated questions pertaining to the advisability of roles as a psychological study. Roles are sociological structures in society. The listing of roles a person assumes or aspires to assume in his life is unproductive for psychological inquiry. Roles become important to a psychologist when the focus changes from roles and their attendant "behavior" to a study of the dynamics underlying role behavior. The differences in behavioral responses may vary as a function of self, others, motivation, and the basis of reality. Roles can provide the individual with the opportunity to be what he wants or to be as others expect him. A role is a means through which an individual can place his cognitions regarding self into "being" by enabling his self-conceptualizations to be made manifest. But the role itself is not a determiner of the self-meaning of an individual. It is through the social role that the individual can reality test his conceptualizations by role taking behavior. Reality in the form of others participating in a social act provides feedback information as to the effects, merits, or benefit of the identity concept to the individual.

Since cognitive functioning is assumed to be an ongoing process, self-as-process is a continuous development. Cognitions are capable of integration and reorganization for generating new interpretations of self that are a function of prior experiences, present cues, and future postulated conditions.

Concept formation is a cognitive function that continues throughout the life of a psychologically intact organism. Therefore, the concepts a person constructs that relate to himself are capable of change. The behavior produced also is susceptible to change. But some identity conceptualizations have importance and are integrated into other concepts. This produces the contancy or perpetuation of some concepts over time and across situations.

Two interviewees summarized their self-as-process by saying,

> I'll be frustrated as long as I'm resigned to the fact I'll never be in a stage of completion.

and

> I'm so much different today than ten years ago, it's a dynamic process.

Chapter 14

Hypothetico-Deductive Statements for Theory of Self-as-Process

ANY SYSTEM OF ORGANIZING IDEAS, such as the building of a theory, not only incorporates givens and observations of the phenomenon under discussion, but includes inferences as well. The givens of self-theory, discussed in the preceding chapters, are basic premises of (a) self-as-process and (b) the structuring of development and operation of the process. Observations of self-as-process were related to products of cognitive-affective activity as concept formations manifested in certain role behaviors. These observations were described and presented in Chapter 13 as illustrative comments of self-involvement in roles, and the effects of identities upon role behaviors. However, the combination of givens and observances with inferences creates a theory and the postulation of inferential statements becomes the subjective, personal, deductive element which helps to formulate a theoretical position.

Inferences of Self-as-Process

Three inferences of self-as-process are:

Inference I. Self-process develops over time throughout the life experiences of the individual. The criterion by which such a statement can be made must be related to the probability that the assumption is based on enough evidence and repeated confrontations with circumstances to lend credence and support to the statement. In this theory substantiation for the above assumption can be abstracted from the "subsystems" that are operative during the progression of the self-process. These subsystems are derived from cognitive-affective bases in the form of identity concepts and their exemplifications in role behaviors. This statement indicates that cognitive development is a fundamental process inherent in self-development. The term process implies that conditional change is integral to the system; that the progress is amenable to change over time, and, that when process includes progression, it infers a directionality in the form of a potential of the system.

Inference II. Concept formations of the self-process are the identity concepts an individual organizes concerning instances of self-references and self-representations processed by integration and differentiation of prior experiences. Instances of self are developmentally integrated and organized and are modified by other factors.

Some observations concerning this assumption are obtained from the discussions with interviewees described in the preceding chapter. Their histories indicated multiple interrelationships of behavioral responses, contextual factors, and self-needs and perceptions of self-other demands as modifying identity concepts throughout life. At specific points in time, certain identity concepts postulated by them were also substantiated by others. These identity concepts were recallable in contexts, (e.g., actions, behaviors, or events) and were discussed as self-exemplified in situational contexts. Through time, identity concepts were modified in terms of their importance and became interrelated with other identity concepts. The process of integrating, interrelating, and reintegrating identity concepts created broader structuring of interpretations of themselves.

Inference III. The structuring of self-meaning is assumed to occur through the postulation of an identity assemblage. The identity assemblage is both organizing and organizer of identity concepts and role relationships together with all processed feedback[1] that went into making an identity concept from a self-referent experience.

Thus, the identity assemblage is not just a self-image, or an evaluation of one's self, or one's values, but is the organizing activity that permits interrelations of identity concepts giving definition and meaning to the individual across situations, specific to the moment and to future conditional contexts and events. In other words, the identity assemblage is more than just the sum of identity concepts; it is the interrelating, processing, and organizing process of self-experiences. This structure (a hypothetical construction) involves the assumption that identity concepts are hierarchically organizable into systems in which those identity concepts or sets of identity concepts more vital or important (at any time) become salient. With self-as-process the organization of the assemblage or structuring of self[2] precludes the permanent rigidity or completeness to an organization of identity concepts. This error is prevented when the assemblage is viewed as organizing potential orderings of relationships of identity concepts as self-reference loci, enabling interpretations of one's own meaning to be derived. The assemblage operates continuously throughout life by reintegrating identity concepts and differentiating meanings of self. Thus, James' (1890) comment that self is the sum of different roles is an incomplete explanation of self-as-process because it does not explain the integration of identity concepts and roles, or the differentiation of meanings of self from all the roles to which James alludes.

Viewing self-as-process, attention shifts from identity concepts as an end product or from focus on *a* self-concept or *an* identity (e.g., Erikson, 1950) to the process of identity con-

---

[1] Weiner (1954) refers to feedback of information as "resulting in adjustive performance," creating possible "multiple contingencies" and also creating variations of behavioral manifestations and contextual applications.

[2] Korzybski (1951) discusses structure in terms of relationships, stating that to have structure one needs a complex or network of ordered and interrelated parts.

ceptualization (building through process of integrating and differentiating cognitive constructions) and exemplification of identity concepts in roles. This becomes a process of cognitive-affective integration and differentiation of meanings of self over time.

Self-as-process changes the focus of study from behavior as an end in itself, by which self is a resultant by-product of behavior, to the view that self-as-process is inherent in creating or initiating certain behavioral responses and is an integral function of cognitive developmental activity. Therefore, a self-as-process position changes the question of inquiry from, "Does man have *a* self?" to, "How does man know himself and give himself definition and meaning?" In this manner, self-as-process is the study of cognitive-affective developmental behavior in which the locus of reference is the organism.

However, the purpose of this chapter is not limited to a restatement of basic premises and inferences of a theory of self but includes (a) the presentation of inductive and deductive statements pertaining to a theory of self-as-process in human development and (b) the implications of these statements for the man who is scientifically curious.

One method of gaining evidence for supporting or refuting the assumptions upon which self-as-process was based was the semi-structured, in-depth interview technique. This technique was useful in supplying direction as to which variables may or may not be important or influential to the process. It provided suggestions for hypothetico-deductive statements relating to self-theory and role behaviors.

Data from the interview method illustrated that interviewees were able to discuss various role behaviors differentially related to self, other persons, motivation, reflexiveness, and reality. Although with retrospective statements one cannot assign complete credibility to the reasons given in self-analysis of behavior, the writers' intent has not been to provide cause and effect data on normality and pathology of self-development of specific individuals. The purpose, rather, is to observe if within individuals certain processes do occur, and whether changes, consistencies, continuities or discontinuities of process can be discerned. Therefore, individual differences are not of concern. What is significant is whether general principles of developmental phenomena occur.

The Focus of Self-Theory

Historically, a discussion limited to a description of positional roles, instead of self in role behavior theory, resulted in a "backward" type, or post hoc, analysis. In other words, if identity concepts are postulated as primary conditional factors in manifesting role behaviors, then identity concepts plus the modifying conditions postulated in Chapter 10 should be the locus of inquiry. However, the historical approach has been to regard overt behavior in positional roles, *per se*. A study of roles had been thought to enable prediction and description of identity concepts of any individual. Post hoc analysis, by studying a list of adopted social roles and forming a breakdown of expected behaviors, leads to a reasoning *cul-de-sac*, for observable behavior may be the manifestation of identity concepts, or a set of identity concepts, anti-identities, or may be unrelated to the self-process as activity manifested in the form of organismic reactions or habit.

The question becomes, "How is the study of a behavioral response able to specify the underlying conditions for its occurrence?" The position taken by the writers is that the study of self in role behavior should not be directed towards an end product (the observable activity phenomenon) only, but toward defining and controlling for the qualifying conditions constituting the genesis for role behavior.

Self-as-process theory subsumes three role postulates and their corollary statements. These postulates were presented in Chapter 10 and pertain to role taking, role playing, and role figmenting behaviors. Role behaviors were differentially dependent upon the effects of self, others, motivation and the locus of control, and reality and reflexiveness as conditional factors qualifying the involvement of self in roles.

In essence, credibility for the postulates and their corollaries was acquired through the methodology of personal inquiry. Interview comments provided insights insofar as they enabled new questions to be formulated, and deductive and inductive statements to be generated.

Perhaps the fundamental problem facing a developmental psychologist is discerning whether the process is continuous through the life spans of individuals; and, if the process is discontinuous, does that discontinuity necessarily denote a pathology? The problem of consistency or constancy is also one of differentiating whether the process becomes a pathological, rigidifying development or whether constancy is a function of normal progression.

The problem of consistency or constancy lies either with the process or within the components of the process. The components of self-as-process are identity concepts, referred to as the contents of the process, and their manifestation in role behavior, referred to as products of the self-process. The primary set of deductions to be derived from self-theory and role behaviors are:

> *Primary Deduction I*   The process of self is a continuous process throughout the life span of the individual.
>
> *Primary Deduction II*   The inconsistency in self-as-process occurs because components (identity concepts and role behaviors) are constantly changing or are a function of change throughout the process due to the ecology of self and environments.

These deductions generate the following inductions for self-theory:

> *Induction IA*   When the process of self is discontinuous, normal development of self is interfered with.
>
> > *Induction IA$_1$*   This will result in a discontinuous self-process or in a pathology of self-continuity and self-orientation with a loss of interpretation of spatial and temporal location of prior experiences to present self-definition and meaning. This condition results from disintegration of self-meanings.

Deductive Statements

The following statements are presented as additional deductions from role theory as a function of self-process, *derived from Deduction I.*

> *Deduction IA*   With development certain continuities of self-as-process are evidenced.
>
> > *Deduction IA$_1$*   Continuities of self-process are due to cognitive affective interpretations of experiences and integration of present information processed in terms of self.

> *Deduction IA₂* Experiences are integrated, organized, and interpreted in terms of the individual's needs and value system as his frame of self-reference.
>
> *Deduction IB* With development, there are certain inconsistencies due to non-continuities in observed behaviors in the form of specific enactment in roles.
>
> > *Deduction IB₁* Behavior inconsistencies are due to interactions of self and environment.
> >
> > > $IB_{1.1}$ Behavior inconsistencies are due to changes in physical, physiological and cognitive development of the individual.
> > >
> > > $IB_{1.2}$ Behavior inconsistencies also are due to changes in social, situational and contextual demands.

A second group of deductions relate to the constancy of the components of the process as *derived from Deduction II.*

> *Deduction IIA* Identity concepts are capable of being integrated and systematized into meaning fields.
>
> *Deduction IIB* Identity concepts are reintegrated and interpreted as self-definitions and can be both situation specific and generalized across situations.
>
> > *Deduction IIB₁* Generalizability of identity concepts across situations assumes saliency of some identities.
> >
> > *Deduction IIB₂* Specificity of identity concepts assumes that some identity concepts are specifically manifested in certain contexts.

Discussion of Deduction II Derivatives

The preceding statements are deduced from data compiled from interview sessions. At certain times, individuals were capable of both giving a broad self-meaning type of interpretation and relating specific identity concepts as a reason for particular role taking behavior. They were able to give a generalized meaning of self and to describe what a certain role situation meant in terms of specific identity concepts exemplified in the role taking behavior. The question is, "Is this ability a function of higher cognitive operational levels or does this type of 'double' self-understanding occur at all cognitive developmental levels?" It is the inclination of these writers that this is the process of concept formation. Earlier in development when event specific behavior is performed, these self-referent "instances" are organized to form primary self-conceptualizations. As self-concept formations, they are amenable to ordering and classification according to separate meaning dimensions depending upon the demands of the situation. Later, with development, identity concepts can be interrelated and reintegrated to generate multiple meanings of self, containing the condition that more salient identity concepts remain integral to self-meaning.

The types of responses given by interviewees appear to be a function of both the structuring of an identity assemblage and the positing of specific identity concepts exemplified in role taking behaviors. Many identity concepts can be exemplified in an available social role through role taking behaviors.

Thus a study of roles confined to or focused on specific expected overt behavioral responses would be fruitless in attempting to discern the underlying factors that initiated the response. A role of "student" becomes a superficially similar social outlet for many identity concepts. It may be an observable manifestation of both role taking and role playing phenomena or it may be unrelated to the role figmented behavior of the individual occurring at that moment.

Inductive Statements

The previous group of deductions lead to the postulation of the following inductive statements as qualifiers of the postulates of role behavior.

> *Induction IIA   Role behavior* is a phenomenon emanating from multiple bases. The focus of each form of role behavior is directed towards positional and status roles. *Roles* are socially expected responses but the manifestation of a specific quality of behavior is determined by the primary conditions of role behavior postulates.
>
> *Induction IIA₁* Many identity concepts can be tested through a similar role.
>
> *Induction IIB*   Satisfaction of others' demands for as-

suming a social role can be achieved by efficient performance of appropriate responses. Roles may be either related to identity concepts or to anti-identities.

Induction IIB₁ There is less variability in available social roles than in the underlying factor in the self-process that initiates the response.

IIB₁.₁ Social context is a modifying factor to variability in role opportunities available or permitted.

IIB₁.₂ The greater variability of components in self-process (identity concepts) with respect to variety of permissible, available roles, produces discontinuous behavior over time, even though the process of self is a continuous process.

Induction IIB₂ The availability of roles causes disjunctive or disruptive behavior over time for certain positional roles are available only in different periods of the life span of the individual.

IIB₂.₁ The disruptive influencers on roles are determined by the following factors:

2.11 the developmental level of the individual

2.12 the meaning of the role to the individual

2.13 situational demands for the role response

2.14 value system of the individual

2.15 reality base for role performance

2.16 source of motivation for role assumption or locus of control of behavior.

These statements emanate from the underlying premise of this theory that the dynamics of the self-process, exemplified by the forms of role behavior, cannot be studied by the recording of positional or status roles. The results of coding self with roles assumes a 1:1 ratio of identity concepts with roles. In such a ratio, assumed, ascribed, and aspired roles are related separately and distinguishable only in specific identity concepts. For such an arrangement to exist, each role must be traced to an identity concept, or each identity concept must be exemplified by a particular social role. From results of interview statements the hypothesized isomorphic relationship (or ratio) of identity concept to role must be refuted. Anecdotal references have shown that any number of hypothesized identity concepts, and previously substantiated identity concepts, are capable of being manifested in the same social role. The role becomes the means to exemplify the *same* identity concept over time and *different* identity concepts than those that previously had been manifested. The variety of self-exemplifications that become possible can create a difference in overt behavioral responses by an individual during a social act.

Hypothetico-Deductive Statements of Self, Roles, and Role Behavior

A summary of hypothetico-deductive statements pertaining to self-as-process theory is presented.

> *Deduction IIIA* Forms of role behavior are an available means for enhancing self-process development by permitting exemplification, testing and subtantiation of identity concepts.
>
> *Deduction IIIB* Role behavior is not synonymous with, nor identical to, roles.
>
>> *Deduction IIIB₁* Role behavior refers to the methods used by an individual as functions of both observable and unobservable cognitive-affective activity, and/or for enhancing the development of self-as-process.
>>
>> *Deduction IIIB₂* Roles refer to specific ascribed and prescribed behaviors emitted during a social act and are differentially determined by a form of role behavior.
>
> *Deduction IIIC* A study limited to social roles cannot arrive at a study of self-as-process.
>
>> *Deduction IIIC₁* Roles are convergent responses for self-process components.
>>
>> *Deduction IIIC₂* Roles are conditional with and limited by social and personal factors.
>
> *Deduction IIID* Role behaviors are process forma-

tions that are dependent upon the factors relating to self, others, motivation, reality, and reflexiveness as discussed in Chapter 10. These factors affect role behavior through personal and social effects.

Deduction IIID$_1$ The level of cognitive development qualitatively changes the type of behavior manifested by the individual by changing his understanding and meaning of role demands.

Deduction IIID$_2$ The variety and availability of social opportunities for each individual changes the observable manifestations of self-products due to needs and appropriateness to self and society.

Deduction IIID$_3$ Continuous identity conceptualizations and reintegrations of cognitive-affective processing of the individual's experiences are necessary for development of self-components.

Deduction IIID$_4$ A value system molds the structuring of identity assemblage by restricting the exemplification of self from certain roles when specific behavioral responses are required which are at variance with the individual's acceptable modes of conduct.

Deduction IIID$_5$ The locus of control of behavior conditions or qualifies the type of behavior the individual will manifest and his personal involvement in a social act.

Implications for Further Study

A beneficial result of theorizing and analysis of attendant research is the opening of new possibilities for study or for clarifying and specifying tacit assumptions. The following statements are recommended for scientific inquiry. They result from interpretation of data and are viewed as potential generators of hypotheses for study of self and role behaviors.

Potential Hypotheses and Inquiries

1. When contexts are less specific as to role demands, role taking behavior becomes more flexible and gen-

eralized as to possible identity concepts manifestation.

2. As situational contexts are more specific, the individual displays behavioral consistency in assumed roles.
3. Certain roles are situation specific.
4. With age, individuals develop greater availability of reference groups permitting a wider social context for positing, exemplifying, and resubstantiating identity concepts.
   4.1 Reference groups availability reaches an optimal level controlled by:
      4.11 age factors
      4.12 social restrictions
      4.13 cultural norms
      4.14 personal value system
5. In familiar groups a person more readily engages in role taking behavior.
6. In new groups or contexts a person usually attempts role playing conforming or fulfilling perceived role expectations.
   6.1 New situations can also be perceived as constituting potential threats to organized self-meaning.
7. Role behaviors are not opposable behaviors in the cognitive-affective development of the individual but become more efficient in interpersonal interaction with decentrism and reciprocity.
   7.1 Role playing and role taking behaviors are necessary for the development of empathy.
   7.2 Role playing as a social learning experience is interdependent with role taking and provides knowledge of role requirements by defining the limits of the person's social world as imposed by self and society.
   7.3 Role playing experiences increase interpersonal adjustment.
8. Stability of personal meaning and adaptability of self in contexts occurs with age.
   8.1 The stability of self-meaning is conditional with social environmental stability.
   8.2 Constancy of social environment reaches optimal adaptability levels.

      8.21   Beyond optimal levels personal adjustment requires a rearrangement of identity concepts into new meanings or discontinuity of self-meaning as self-interpretation occurs.

9.   Through role figmenting behavior, an individual can broaden his association with reference groups, freeing situational contexts from space-time-reality limitations.

      9.1   Through role figmenting behavior a person can emulate a role model by conceptualizing identity concepts similar to those symbolizing the role figure in his cognitive constructions. The role figure is interpreted as representing important self-attributes hypothesized or posited as desirable or needed but which are at the time incapable of manifestation as an exemplified identity concept.

      9.2   Role figmenting behavior can eliminate the process of positing identity conceptualizations and obtaining substantiation by others in reality contexts through imaginary and pretense conditions for accepting cognitive constructions.

10.   If roles are forms of social responsibility and individual responsibility in society, what is the effect on an individual's adjustment when the major salient identity concepts are exemplified through a specific social role? Does that individual run a greater risk of potential self-disorientation when the social role is no longer permitted than the individual who has compartmentalized or differentially clustered concepts into a variety of social roles?

11.   What is the need, effect, or influence of role surrogates at different developmental periods of an individual's life in terms of demands and expected social tasks?

12.   A study of fantasy and play behavior should be undertaken to define theoretically what factors emerge, to discern that imitative, repetitive, imaginary, and pretense behaviors are developmentally determined and cognitively differentiated in relation to role behaviors.

13. Infant observations have led investigators to suggest that reinforcement for actions is not necessarily a function of external reinforcement but may be a function of internal motivation of mastery or competence between doing the act and the effects of the act. The effects of an individual's behaviors are reinforcing if they are caused by the individual's own initiated activity, and the action is satisfying, if it leads to mastery. Intrinsic motivation of behavior should increasingly come under the control of social reinforcement with age. This assumption involves further development and usage of role playing with age, to accommodate to social demands rather than focusing solely on meeting and satisfying self-demands in reality contexts. However, maximum usage of role playing is assumed to be reached in early adolescence. During this period propositional thinking and hypothetical-deductive thinking should both elicit and modify exemplifications of self in role taking behavior by restricting the quality of manifestations by the imposition of values.

14. People in series of contextual situations require many different role behavior manifestations. By accommodating to reference "others" who expect different behaviors, people will manifest many different concepts of self through role taking behaviors. W. James (1890) said that a person has a somewhat different "self" for every social relationship in which he is found. Weinstein (1965) also suggests that some individuals are adept at interpreting situations and establishing special positions in those situations to achieve confirmations of desired "concepts" of self. These identity concepts may be temporary as self-manifested in specific situations and used as a means of achieving a self-need or purpose. Would a person's social perception or social "intelligence" be a function of the variety of role behavior experiences? Would role experiences enable that person to perform in accordance with social expectations by manifesting specific identity concepts that will satisfy both social and self-needs and substantiate identity concepts important to a specific self-meaning?

15. If role figmenting behavior is a function of self-initiated covert activity, then competence in one's own activity is intrinsic motivation. It is speculated that role figmenting behavior is an attempt of the individual to establish meaning of its own organism through subjective, egocentric dialogue, and is not synonymous with a "dependency" motivation of imitative and incorporative behavior.

This list presents just a brief sample of items for inquiry and as generating potential hypotheses relating to the theory of self-as-process and to the hypothetico-deductive statement derived from self and role behaviors.

Self-as-process is the process that underlies the personal involvement of the individual in his world. Identity formations conceptualized throughout the cognitive-affective development of an individual, as manifested in certain role behaviors, are changing, flexible components of the process.

An increasing ability to integrate, differentiate, and reintegrate identity concepts, and to interpret self-meaning in terms of processed feedback, enables increasing the individual's adaptability to various contextual situations. By means of integration and organization of experiential encodings, a variety of specific interpretations of self can be made. However, substantiation of certain identity concepts by others in a variety of contexts gives saliency to these identity concepts and provides a constancy factor to the derivable self-meanings over time and across situations. Thus, to each individual, "self" becomes his own reference for all his experiences, attitudes, and potentials, and is the means he uses to refer to and to define his own organism and his behavior. But each person can perceive only a part of all his conceptual possibilities at any point in time, resulting in the limitation and selectivity of his scope of total self-awareness.

Chapter 15

Reprise

Of all man's attributes *self* appears to be the most complex, yet most intangible. Self is man's most essential enterprise, the only reality he has, representing a process of viewing and editing both his own and external stimuli. Self is a necessary development, for it is a mediating process which presents, interprets, and defines environmental effects as they occur at a moment or are assumed to exist in the past and future with the locus of reference for the process being the individual. Self is a personal reference construct involving a cognitive-affective or perceiving-interpreting action system possessing the attribute of awareness. This process operates on the basis of expectancies and hypotheses formulated as a result of actual and vicarious learnings from processing of experiences. Self-concepts are cognitive-affective constructions and represent inner views capable of being projected to external environments for feedback and evaluation. Self-process consists of the total constructions that an attending, observing individual places upon his own entity and its interactive effects with surrounding contexts.

Self-process consists of conceptualizations derived from experience, representing interpretations and assumptions in various temporal-spatial contexts as the individual seeks the meaning of himself and his relatedness to his world. Self-as-process is continuous throughout the life of a psychologically intact individual, consisting of cognitive conceptualizations amenable to change and reconstruction.

The first two decades of human life are particularly important, for these are the years when the individual is seeking meaning as an unique entity and establishing a bond of commonality with his contemporaries. These are the years of building, revising, and reintegrating concepts of self and for relating these constructions to the surrounding world of persons and situations. During these stages of development a person tests his self-hypotheses against reality and modifies them by integrating and assessing the feedback he receives to their appropriateness as assumptions of self. During these years events, people, things, and happenings also must be encoded and made meaningful. There is an assimilation of the culture through symbolic representation. Such assimilation furthers the accommodative patterns of adaptation that are integrated to the point of permitting: (a) dependence upon self and interdependence with others, (b) identities which individuate, (c) conceptualizations of paths for purposive, directional, and aspired existence, (d) assumption of responsibility for self and others, and (e) attainment of mature self-love manifested in selflessness or non-possessiveness.

To be operative, self-process must have available a context, a codifying memory schema, differential experience, internal and external interaction, cognitive capacity, feeling, affect, and the ability to qualitatively analyze.

As a developmental process self evolves chiefly from learning, beginning during the uterine months. During these primary sensory-motor interactions cognitive-affective anlagen are formed. Self-process continues throughout the life span of each individual confined within the parameters imposed by his genetic endowments and environmental opportunities. During the operation of self-as-process, cognitive concepts are integrated from previous assessed experiences and structured with accompanying affect. Exemplification of self is the manner in which an individual relates conceptualizations of himself to the reality which surrounds him.

With the emergence of an individual's ability to think symbolically a hierarchy of identities begins to evolve. An identity hierarchy is an assemblage of self-hypotheses reaching fruition as a structuring of self-products when an individual develops the ability for hypothetical-deductive reasoning. With propositional thinking he is able to hypothesize identities, test them against reality and interrelate identities for possible self-meanings.

In some cases a specific identity may be exteriorized to some person or object in the actual or imagined environment which will, in effect, stand surrogate for a particular aspect of the exteriorized self. For that aspect of self, the exteriorizer denies the reality of the non-self entity and perceives it as in unity with his conceptualization of self.

Self and identities are not synonymous. Self-process involves the integration and differentiation of a multiplicity of identities. Identities are cognitively synthesized from concepts of self and are capable of reconstruction by modification, reintegration, and combination with other self-hypotheses.

Self-concepts develop over the years of childhood as an individual transmutes drives and physiological tension states into elaborated needs through a process of socialization. Ultimately the developing individual builds a system of purposive behavior based on directionality, engendered by elaborated needs and a value system. Early needs are hedonic and prerequisite for the viability of the organism with self-exemplary needs making a later appearance.

In the human developmental cycle physiological tensions are important for the development of somatic percepts of self. As the psychic concepts of self take a dominant position through development of symbolic representations, elaborated needs ascend in importance in the self-process until the emergence of values as directives for behavior and desired end states. During late adolescence, when propositional thinking can occur, values gain primacy and serve to mold the identity assemblage and influence manifestation of identities in roles. Those identities in adult life of highest significance to the individual are representative of the values held and take precedence in the behavioral performances of the person. The development and operation of self-process are incomprehensible without giving consideration to the effects of the individual's values system. But, as age takes its toll during senescence, psychic as well as physical deterioration occurs. The effects of the value system upon behavior and structuring of identities yields precedence to physiological tensions and hedonic needs, and, to a lesser extent, to the elaborated needs.

Deterioration is the last phase of the developmental cycle as the individual returns to an earlier state. But even before this last stage there is a phasing effect. Dabrowski (1964) speaks of the cyclic nature of development with disintegration occurring when too great complexity is reached, at which point the system reverts back to a simpler order after which it can go forward again. Werner (1948) speaking of orthogenesis notes that in development there is regression before forward progress can be achieved. Such phasing in life offers a partial explanation for the stress conditions in transition periods, manifested as negativism or egocentricity.

During the period of their primacy, values are expressed in the form of attitudes and behavioral outcomes reciprocally with identities in the forms of role taking behavior. With role experiences, as a result of social learning, each person develops behavior styles. The appearance of behavior styles is governed by what an individual sees as appropriate for the structure of his society and the demands of the role as well as appropriate to his self-needs and his system of value. His various accommodative behaviors to role opportunities are differentially related to his self-process, others' expectations, a reality basis and a reflexive nature of feedback, and to motivation and locus of control. These conditions modify the involvement of identities in roles, forming role taking, role playing, and role figmenting behaviors.

Through exterior figure socialization the child assigns roles to various representative figures and builds a picture of his social world. For this role representative, he structures behavior attributes and learns the behavioral expectations required for a role assumption. By forming concepts of others in roles, his perceptions of behavioral requirements influence how he reacts to them and his self-conceptualizations are, in turn, influenced by the way they respond to him. Their reactions are encoded as affective feedback modifying his concepts of self. Parents, parent surrogates, peer and reference groups are of particular importance to his self-evaluations. They are typically structured in compatible or interactive roles.

Some of the conflicts in periods of transition, such as adolescence, are dependent upon the resolution of identity diffusion and role confusions. The individual who resolves his "identity crises" has to regroup or reintegrate concepts of self and hypothesize identities for testing in roles that will lend feasibility to them as self-references. Role confusion arises when identities successfully performed in one role are not appropriately received in another and depend upon the individual learning the expectations of others for acceptable demand behaviors in role performance in situational specific contexts.

Life sequence includes periods of negativism in early childhood, in adolescence, and in old age. Negativism stems from environmental blocking of manipulative and mastery needs and from the difficulty encountered in attempting to exemplify self in reality contexts.

Another important impact of self-process involves self-esteem. An individual's choices, self-evaluations, and self-perceptions depend upon his self-esteem as determined by the standards he has set for evaluating his self-concepts. Attitudes differ in context, direction, importance, salience, consistency, stability, and clarity; each person classifies his concepts on the basis of these dimensions. Values ascribe criteria and standards for modes of behavior and for end states of existence.

An individual's cognitive development makes him capable of behavior of increasing complexity as he grows older. The complexity of an individual's concepts of self and his ability to hypothesize identities is limited by the level of cognitive development he has attained as well as by the diversity of role experiences he has encountered.

Cognition is a process whereby an organism becomes aware or obtains knowledge of an object. In developmental psychology cognition is primarily considered in terms of concept formation, problem solving, and the thought processes. Any individual builds a conceptual system through which he views both himself and the world. Developmentally, the issue deals with the level of cognitive manipulation available to the individual as he builds his self-system. As the individual grows older his movement is toward greater abstract behavior as he passes through the various levels of cognitive behavior. Particularly helpful in understanding self-process is the four-stage sequential theory of mental growth advanced by Piaget. Of the four stages, the fourth, occurring during adolescence, describes much of the behavior process that must occur as the individual enters the most crucial stages in his formation of concepts of self. During the fourth stage, the individual must no longer confine himself to perceived data from his immediate temporal and spatial environment. His thinking becomes propositional, and he possesses the capacity to interrelate ideas and suppositions. The formal operations of the fourth stage are applied to hypotheses or assumptions, while the concrete operations of the third stage are applied to tangible objects or perceivable events. Central to an understanding of the fourth stage of cognitive growth is the picture of the individual as a hypothesizing, systematizing organism. As he enters the fourth stage he once again displays considerable egocentricity, but with increasing maturity he leaves this egocentricity as he comes to perceive that the proper function of reflection is to predict and interpret experience and to posit alternatives, not merely to contradict.

Answering the question "Who am I?" is one way to gain insight into the relative structuring of an identity hierarchy. Identities are the individual's guide to the roles he takes that satisfy self-needs and are appropriate to the expectation of society if substantiation of them as self-references is to be gained. Identities dictate the manner in which an individual will handle or behave in roles he accepts for himself. The roles he plays, while not involving identities, are evaluated as performance of behavioral requirements of the demands of society. Other roles may be figmented permitting the person to fantasize or imagine possible, although not necessarily probable, conceptualizations of self in non-reality contexts. The figmenting role behavior permits trying out roles without the intervention of reality. Since reality would have an inhibiting effect on taking a role, imagination or pretense behavior permits the role to be assumed.

While self-concepts change and are reintegrated during adolescence, a tendency toward establishing self-meaning becomes increasingly strong in later years by the structuring of identities in the assemblage into a flexible hierarchy. This is particularly evident when the manifestation of self-hypothesis has been satisfactorily met in roles and is resubstantiated by interactive experiences, offering a satisfactory self-view in which the individual has confidence.

A major developmental task is the attainment of a sense of responsibility if the individual is to become a socially useful person of maximum use to himself and accountable to himself and others for his actions. Agencies of society should endeavor to permit a sense of personal and social responsibility to develop in children they rear if optimum results in terms of self-acceptance and social adaptability are to ensue.

When all is said and done, building self-concepts is a very personal task although the context in which they are evaluated is essentially a social one. Thus, self becomes a multiple of references man creates to refer to and to define his own organism and the effects of his behavior. Self consists of all the permutations and integrations of a person's experiences and potentials. At any point in time, a person can perceive and evaluate only a small part of all that he can conceive himself to be. To assume that each individual can, at any given time in his life, perceive his entirety of self-meanings is more than an anomaly; it is an impossibility.

Appendix

Self and Role: Interview Format

I am going to ask you a number of questions concerning attitudes and observations of your youth and adult life. Feel free to expound in any way that you see fit on the questions asked. The ideal situation would be if you can tell me of any instances or facts that come to your mind in relation to the subjects presented to you, and if the situation arises, tell me of any instances or attitudes that you can remember or that you have now. In other words, if you can, answer by illustration.[1]

Structuring of Identity Concepts

Q. Give me the names of your brothers or sisters, their ages, and what relation in age they are to you.

Q. Think of your best friends during childhood and adulthood, and also your closest relatives. These people may be old or young, but are these the people

---

[1] These questions are a guide format only. They are used to initiate discussion of self-references and self-views. The interviewer should direct his comments to the natural flow of conversation. When multiple questions are combined, they should be asked sequentially, to generate additional comments from the interviewee, and to redirect his responses back to his own concepts of self (Jackson, 1970).

you consider to be *close* to you? Tell me who they are and describe them with reference to you.

Q. Thinking of your brothers, sisters, or best friends and relatives, who would you consider most different from you? (Time-period reference to be asked if not stated by interviewee.)

Q. What ways do they differ from you, or what vital and important differences do you see?

Q. Compare yourself with the people you consider most different from you. (Each person named.)

Q. Thinking of your brothers, sisters, best friends and relatives, who was most like you?

Q. How were they like you? (What traits did you see in them that you have?) How do you compare yourself with them?

Q. Who do you think or consider as having played well together?

Q. Who fought and argued with each other?

Q. I realize that in many friendships there usually is a person who looked after or took care of others. Who was that and what did he do that would make you think that he took care of someone? Describe.

Q. Was there any illness, such as surgery, broken bones, etc. in your family (include interviewee also) or among your close friends that in some way affected you?

Q. Thinking of the basic list that we started out with, was there anyone or anything that you considered to be strange or uncommon, and if so, how?

Q. Considering the list (or anyone at all) who did you consider to be the friendliest, and what made them friendly? Compare yourself with that person.

Q. Who was the most intelligent or smartest person that you knew or know? Compare yourself with that person.

Q. Who did you consider as the person who made the best grades in school? Then compare yourself with that person.

Q. What was your favorite subject in school, or what did you like to study while in school? What made you like that particular subject?

Q. What was the subject that you liked least, or the subjects that you didn't like to study in school? What made you dislike those subjects?

Q. Who would you consider to be the most industrious person, and the one who worked the hardest? What, in your mind, made him seem industrious to you? Then compare yourself with that person.

Q. Who did you feel got things done? Give me an illustration. Compare yourself with that person.

Q. What person did the most work or helped the most, and where, e.g., at home or school, work? Give an illustration and compare yourself with that person.

Q. We know of a number of people we consider as having the most complaints or who "cry" the most. Tell me about a person like this and then compare yourself with this person.

Q. There are some people who say things wrong most of the time, and always seem to get into problems because of this. Do you know of any? If so, tell me the type of things that they probably do say. Compare yourself with this person (if the interviewee did *not* describe himself).

Q. Who do you know who says that he is always unhappy? (Illustrate, if you can, and then compare yourself with that person.)

Q. Who do you know who feels that life is rather unfair to him, a person who complains most? Tell me what he is like, and then compare yourself with him.

Q. In every group we know that there are one or two people who appear to quarrel the most. Do you know of such a person? Give me an illustration, if you can, and then compare yourself with that person.

Q. Who do you know that sulks the most? What makes him sulk? Compare yourself with that person.

Q. What person do you know that causes the most mischief, either because he wants to or because he just does? Give me an illustration, and then compare yourself with that person.

Q. Thinking again of your friends and family (past and present), who would you say is the most conforming or most obedient? How are you like or unlike the person?

Q. Every family has a certain set of values that is more or less spelled out to them in their youth. In thinking of your family, what were the values that were important to your family? What were those things that were not allowed by your parents? Did you conform? How? Was and is there anything that you did or do not conform to?

Q. I am sure that you know people who are openly rebellious, people who never did things that other people wanted them to. Do you know such a person? Describe, and then tell me how or in what ways you are like or unlike that person.

Q. Many people don't like to be bossed around, and yet there are some who can take it and some who can't. Who do you know that doesn't like to be bossed around? What particularly irks him? Illustrate, if possible, and then compare yourself with that person. How did you react in a specific situation?

Q. Who do you recall appeared to be punished the most; for instances, was yelled at, whipped, or spanked? Who was this punishment administered by, and for what reasons? How did you compare?

Q. We all feel that we, at one time or another, have been picked on and we often feel sorry for ourselves; but who do you recall who appeared to be picked on

and felt more sorry for himself than normal?
Compare yourself with that person.

Q.   Who do you consider to be a moody person? Do you
consider yourself moody, in comparison? How, or
why not?

Q.   In any family or group situation, moods effect others.
Was the rest of the family influenced by your moods?
How?

Q.   Who could you make unhappy with your moods? Did
you go out of your way to cause anyone unhappiness?

Q.   When you got into a particular mood, whom did you
pick on or react to and why?

Q.   Thinking of all your friends, who was the most popular with the others? (What made him popular? How
did you compare?)

Q.   Who was the most easygoing with the others? What
made him appear easygoing? How do you compare?

Q.   Many of us like to be by ourselves, but some prefer
it more than others. Who do you remember as liking
to be by himself? (Compare yourself with that person.)

Q.   In every group there is a person who goes out of his
way to please others and tries to do things that make
other people happy. Do you know such a person?
What can you remember that would give you this
impression? (Compare yourself.)

Q.   Think of a person always critical of others—someone
who says that other people are not right or are not
good. I am thinking of an over-critical person. Compare yourself with that person.

Q.   An attribute that some people have is their consideration to others. Think of someone you consider
in this vein and then compare yourself with that
person.

Q.   Selfishness is a trait that most of us have to some
extent. Who do you know whom you would consider

to be selfish, a person that wants everything for himself? What do you think makes him selfish? (Compare yourself to this person.)

Q. Many people easily get their feelings hurt, and are considered to be sensitive. Think about a sensitive person you know and describe him in terms of this feeling. (Compare yourself with him.)

Q. Who always wants his own way, and demands his own way? Describe these demands. (Compare yourself with this person.)

Q. Who do you know who gets his own way, seems to be the most independent, or does things when he feels like doing them? Describe. (Compare yourself.)

Q. Some of us are considered to have quite a temper. Tell me about someone that gets mad easily. (Compare yourself.)

Q. A sense of humor is most important. Tell me about someone you consider to have a good sense of humor—one who laughs a lot. How do you rate in humor, compared with this person?

Q. Who do you know who enjoys making other people laugh? Describe. (How do you compare yourself?)

Q. Think of a person who likes to "yak" it up more than other people, or jokes more than other people. What puts him in this category, as far as you are concerned? (Compare yourself to him.)

Q. Think about a "kid" who is a pleasure to have around and describe him. Do you think you were a pleasure to have around? Be specific, e.g., why, how, and where.

Q. There are all degrees of sweetness, niceness and charm. Who do you know that has the most charm and is the sweetest or nicest toward people? Tell me about him. (Compare yourself.)

Q. Tell me who you consider the easiest to get along with, and what makes him easy to get along with. Do you think you are easy to get along with?

Q. Athletics play an important part in most of our lives. Who do you consider to be the most athletic or good in sports? (Compare yourself.)

Q. I am looking for someone whom you consider to be strong. Tell me what makes that person strong. Do you consider yourself strong in comparison?

Q. Who do you think is the best looking person, either male or female, that you know? Describe this person. Compare yourself and tell me how you are similar or dissimilar.

Q. Idealistic qualities mean different things to different people. Who do you consider to be idealistic? What does idealistic mean to you? Would you consider yourself idealistic? How?

Q. Many people like to possess "materialistic" things. To whom is this important? What type of things does this person possess? Are you "materialistic"? How?

Q. There are different standards of right and wrong, and yet there are some people who always seem to know what is right and wrong, and will always tell you what course to follow. Do you know such a person? Give me an illustration. Do you consider yourself to have a good standard of right and wrong? Tell me about it.

Parental Figures

I am going to ask you a number of questions about your parents. Try to answer them to the best of your ability.

Q. What is the current age of your father? (If deceased, note the age of subject when parent died.)

Q. Who did *you* consider to be your father's favorite child? (Not necessarily based on actuality but on *your perceptions* of the relationship.) Why would you consider that child to be his favorite? Describe a situation(s) that makes you feel that this child was your father's favorite. Who do you think is his favorite now?

Q. All parents have certain ambitions for their children. What was your father's ambition for his children? Did he ever sit down and talk to you about the future for you and his other children? What was your father's relationship to the children, either individually or as a total effect? Describe.

Q. Which sibling was most like your father? In what ways was he like your father? If possible, describe what made you feel that this was so.

Q. Tell me your mother's current age. Who did you think or consider to be your mother's favorite child when growing up? Why do you consider this person to be your mother's favorite? What position did you hold in comparison? Who do you think is your mother's favorite child now?

Q. Did your mother have any pointed ambitions for her children, and did she direct you toward your future goals?

Q. What was your mother's relationship to the children of the family? Describe.

Q. Which sibling was most like your mother? Tell me how you came to this conclusion, or show a situation(s) that happened to make you feel this way.

Q. What was the nature of your parents' relationship? In other words, how did they react to one another, socially and on a personal basis. Describe.

Additional Parental or Adult Figures

Many of us are reared by our parents, and yet we look upon other people as parental figures. This may include aunts, uncles, grandparents, teachers, principals, neighbors—some authority we personally went to for advice or security. Thinking back to your childhood . . .

Q. What person stayed in your memory as a parental figure? What made you choose that person or persons? Describe your relationship to them. (If you didn't have any, what do you think was a reason for this relationship or closeness not to occur in your life?)

Q.   Do you still, if you had parental surrogate figures, keep in contact with them now?

Q.   Thinking of these people, tell me how they substituted for your parents in a particular situation. In other words, for a person(s) other than your parent to give you this feeling, he (they) must have filled some needs. What were these needs?

Q.   Did you belong to clubs as a child? Did you ever participate in these clubs as part of a group, or as an individual? What did you do in these clubs? How did you behave with your group? Is there anything about the club that stands out in your memory?

Q.   In your peer group, what type of persons are you attracted to? What makes them attractive to you, or what did you have in common?

Personal Actions-Reactions-Roles

We realize that we all act differently in different situations, and I am looking for an indication of how you behave or perceive yourself in a specific class or situation.

Q.   How did you react in "class" (e.g., aggressive, defensive, antagonistic, etc.)?

Q.   What kind of a student did you *want* to be? What kind of a student did the *teacher expect* you to be? How do these differ in your estimation?

Q.   When meeting a new girl for the first time, there is a certain image that you want to portray in order to give the new girl a certain impression of you. What do you *wish to convey* about yourself, and how do you go about doing this? In what type situations would you prefer to meet her and why? How do you want her to perceive you, and how do you want her to remember you?

Q. Describe how you put yourself into various situations. Elaborate in incidents or by illustration of yourself in specific interactions.

Q. What are your ideals (standards) for yourself and your behavior with others?

Q. What type or kinds of things would you *like to do* with your life?

Q. What are the kind of things in your life that you see as being very *important* to you?

Q. What type of work would you *like* to be doing ten years from now?

Q. How did you *decide* to go into your various occupations or professions?

Q. How do you see yourself as a __(fill in vocation)__ ?

Q. How do you act with others in the role of __(vocation or avocation)__ ?

Q. What do you perceive are others' demands and expectations of you? (If any, be specific as to *where* and *when* others place these demands upon you.)

Q. Do you differentiate between work and an occupation? If so, how?

Q. What is the image or attitudes that you have about yourself at this point in your life? (Describe or illustrate by instances if possible.)

Q. When you meet a new fellow for the first time, whether he is a peer or on a different level, how do you react to that person? Give examples. What type of an impression do you want to create about yourself, and what type of an attitude do you have toward this new acquaintance?

Q. Some things we are today are based upon something we have from the past, such as attitudes, conceptions, experiences, etc. What do you perceive are the most important relationships or happenings that have made you the type of person that you are today?

Q. What kind of work do you see yourself as doing? Why? What kind of work can you see yourself as *not* doing? Why?

Q. How *important* is work to you?

Q. What do you *expect out* of your work?

Q. If you have a personal legacy to leave behind, how would you *like* to be remembered? How *will* you be remembered?

Q. What are the things that you do not attribute to yourself that others might? In other words, many peoples' analyses of you in a situation may or may not be the way *you actually perceive yourself*. How are their expectations different from what you are?

Q. Can you give me some "recollections" about yourself? Describe in detail what you did (others did, if any), where, when, why it (each one) happened.

Q. You may often find that you dream, and in many cases where work is boring, we daydream. Tell me what your current dreams are, and what is *your part* in the dreams. What is your reaction to your dream when you awaken?

Q. Do you have a recurrent dream(s)? (What are they? Describe.) Were you *in* your dreams?

Q. There are childhood dreams that stick out in your mind. Tell me if you can recall any of them, and your reaction to them.

Q. Do you daydream? What do you imagine yourself doing, or being? Do you have a favorite daydream? What are your fantasies in terms of yourself? Describe how you are involved in your fantasies. What do you do and how does that compare with the way you are in reality?

Q. What type of games did you play as a youngster? What type of games did you play alone, and in a group? Did you initiate the play situations? Were you a follower or a leader in these games? Explain.

Q. Describe yourself in body size, stature, and looks, etc. as a child; and, if you wish, this can cover a number of periods in growing up.

Q. Compare yourself or describe how you see yourself today.

Q. How do you like to *imagine* yourself as looking at the present?

Q. How do you *have to appear* to others in your occupation, recreation, church, and other groups? (In terms of their expectations of you.)

Q. Describe what types of standards you have set (for yourself) in terms of: yourself, your work, your wife, your future, and your life, and whatever else you feel is important to you.

Q. In terms of those things that directly affect the way you see yourself, what are the things you *fear* most?

Q. Compare your childhood fears to your present ones.

Q. Tell me about your childhood ambitions. What did you think you were going to be when you grew up?

Q. Tell me about your present ambitions.

Q. If I were to give you three wishes, what would they be (have been) as a youngster? What would they be now?

Q. Tell me about the most outstanding person or persons you know. What, in your mind, makes them seem outstanding? Compare them to yourself.

Q. Describe your personal assets, those things that make you you. How have you made use of these assets in your everyday life?

Q. There are many things that we do when we don't really want to do them. What do you do that is expected of you, that you *don't really want* to do? Describe.

Q. What are your most important attitudes or beliefs about yourself? Compare these with the way that you see yourself?

At this point I am going to summarize quickly many of the points that we have already covered. What I am attempting to do is to recap some of the points, and you can condense your answers if you wish, or you may want to elaborate further on some of the answers that you gave to my previous questions, since you now have had time possibly to think more about the questions that were presented to you.

Q. Tell me about the pressures that you felt within the family, and tell me about the family atmosphere and their moods.

Q. How did the family attempt to educate you, and also cover the habits, practices, ideas, or values that they instilled in you or passed on to you? How did others influence you in terms of those things you just mentioned?

Q. Give me a general impression of yourself growing up.

Q. Give me a general impression of yourself in relation to others—both growing up and as an adult.

Q. In whom did you confide, and why did you pick that particular person?

Q. Did you ever keep personal notes about anything that has ever happened to you; e.g., a diary, notes, or letters. If these were kept, why did you keep them?

Q. Looking over the years, what do you see as typical of yourself and consistent with the way you see yourself?

Q. What were your impressions of self-frustrations and how have you tried to overcome or cope with them?

Q. Your parents or siblings may consider certain things extremely important, and yet you may not. What is important to them that is not important to you; or what is important to you that is not important to them; and how did you go about achieving your desired results?

Q.   What are some of the responsibilities that you have undertaken?

Q.   What are some of the responsibilities that you are required to fulfill?

Q.   Have you ever, or do you now assume responsibility for others? How?

Q.   Some of us stray from the path taken in our youth. If this applies to you, when did you begin to see a reconciliation or a reconnection with your roots? In other words, have you seen a reconnection from where you began to where you are now?

Q.   In terms of your concepts of self and standards for self, how do you define yourself in terms of good, bad, right, or wrong?

Q.   Has marriage or prospects of marriage altered those things that you feel are important about yourself, or those things that you strive for?

Q.   If something happens to prevent you from being a professional in your field, what else would you be?

Q.   What *would you not* be, under any circumstances? Why?

Q.   You are made up of or hold certain concepts that make you an individual, or that make you you. Of all the things you are, which are the most important percepts or concepts you hold about yourself?

Q.   How do you *feel* about the way you see yourself, in terms of your ideals?

Q.   What are the values of those things by which you gauge or judge how close you come to your ideals?

Q.   In what types of situations do you *not show* people what you are like; e.g., if you are an overly sensitive person, in what situations do you not show this? Explain what you do.

Q. When people demand certain performances from you, how do you overcome or comply with these demands? Why would you do this?

Q. To what extent do you do things that are not really like you? Why? How do *you* feel in performing these expectations?

Q. To what extent do you do things that you really don't want to do, in terms of your concepts of self (e.g., feign interest in a vocation, or act like a leader, or a mediator, or a boss, or dependable when you don't perceive yourself with this quality)?

Q. What are those things that you imagine yourself doing that you haven't been able to do or don't see yourself as doing in real life (e.g., imaginary roles)?

Post Interview

Q. Do you have any additional things you wish to state in reference to yourself, the things you do or the way you are?

Bibliography

Adelson, J., and O'Neil, R. The growth of political ideas in adolescence. *Journal of Personality and Social Psychology*, 1966, *4*:295–306.

Allport, G. W. *Personality: A psychological interpretation.* New York: Holt, 1937.

Ausubel, D. F. *Theory and problems of child development.* New York: Grune and Stratton, 1958.

Backman, C. W., Secord, F. F., and Pierce, J. R. Resistance to change in the self-concept as a function of consensus among significant others. *Sociometry,* 1963, *25*:102–111.

Baldwin, J. M. *Mental development in the child and the race.* New York: Macmillan, 1895.

Bertalanffy, L. von. *Modern theories of development.* London: Oxford University Press, 1933.

Bertalanffy, L. von. *Problems of life.* London: C. A. Watts, 1952.

Biddle, B., and Thomas, E. J. (Eds.) *Role theory: Concepts and research.* New York: Wiley, 1966.

Boring, E. G. *The physical dimensions of consciousness.* New York: Appleton-Century, 1933.

Borsedi, R. The neglected science of values. *Journal of Human Relations,* 1965, *13*:433–445.

Braham, M. Peer group deterrents to intellectual development during adolescence. *Educational Theory,* 1965, *15*:248–258.

Bronson, G. W. Identity diffusion in late adolescence. *Journal of Abnormal and Social Psychology,* 1959, *59*:414–417.

Bruner, J. S., Olver, R. R., and Greenfield, P. M., *et al. Studies in cognitive growth.* New York: Wiley, 1966.

Buhler, C. Earliest trends in goal setting. *Zeitshrift Kinderpsychiatrie,* 1958, *25*:13–23.

Buytendikj, F. Unruhe und Geborgenheit in der Welt des jungen Menschen. *Universitas*, 1958, *13:*721–730.

Cameron, N. *Personality development and psychopathology.* Boston: Houghton Mifflin, 1963.

Cannon, W. B. *The wisdom of the body.* New York: Norton, 1932.

Cernik, H., and Thompson, H. H. Decision making by teen-agers in six problem areas: Response to the problem of choice of mates. *Character Potential*, 1966, *3:*162–168.

Combs, A. W., and Snygg, D. *Individual behavior.* New York: Harper, 1959.

Cooley, C. H. *Human nature and the social order.* New York: Scribner, 1922.

Coopersmith, S. *Antecedents of self-esteem.* San Francisco: W. H. Freeman, 1967.

Cross, H. J. Conceptual systems theory: Application to the problems of the adolescent. *Adolescence*, 1967, *2:*153–164.

Dabrowski, K. *Positive disintegration.* Boston: Little, Brown, 1964.

Dignan, M. H. Ego identity and maternal identification. *Journal of Personality and Social Psychology*, 1965, *1:*476–483.

Dubos, R. Life is an endless give and take with earth and all her creatures. *Smithsonian*, 1970, *1:*9–17.

Edwards, A. L. The relationship between the judged desirability of a trait and the probability that the trait will be endorsed. *Journal of Applied Psychology*, 1953, *37:*90–93.

Edwards, A. L. *Manual for Edwards Personal Preference Schedule.* New York: Psychological Corp., 1954.

Elkin, F. Socialization and the presentation of self. *Marriage and Family Living*, 1958, *20:*320–325.

Elkind, D. Conceptual orientation shifts in children and adolescents. *Child Development*, 1966, *37:*493–498.

Engel, M. The stability of the self-concept in adolescence. *Journal of Abnormal and Social Psychology*, 1959, *58:*211–215.

English, H. B., and English, A. C. *A comprehensive dictionary of psychological and psychoanalytical terms.* New York: Longmans, Green, 1958.

Erikson, E. H. *Childhood and society.* New York: Norton, 1950.

Erikson, E. H. *Childhood and society.* 2nd edition. New York: Norton, 1963.

Erikson, E. H. Youth: Fidelity and diversity. *Daedalus,* 1962, *91*:5–27.

Festinger, L. *A theory of cognitive dissonance.* New York: Harper and Row, 1957.

Fine, P. M., and Jennings, C. L. Coping and developmental theory. *Aeromedical Review,* 1965, No. 1.

Flavell, J. H. *The developmental psychology of Jean Piaget.* Princeton: D. Van Nostrand, 1963.

Frankl, V. E. *From death camp to existentialism.* Boston: Beacon Press, 1959.

Freud, A. Adolescence. *Psychoanalytic study of the child.* Vol. 13, International University Press, 1958.

Freud, S. *The psychopathology of everyday life.* New York: Macmillan, 1904.

Fromm, E. *The art of loving.* New York: Harper and Row, 1956.

Gardner, R. W. Cognitive controls in adaptation: Research and measurement. In Messick, S. and Ross, S. *Measurement in personality and cognition.* New York: Wiley, 1962.

Gardner, R. W. The development of cognitive structures. In Scheerer, C. (Ed.) *Cognition: Theory, research, promise.* New York: Harper and Row, 1964.

Gerard, H. B. Some determinants of self-evaluation. *Journal of Abnormal and Social Psychology,* 1961, *62*:288–293.

Gesell, A. *The embryology of behavior: The beginnings of the human mind.* New York: Harper, 1945.

Gesell, A., Ilg, F. L., and Ames, L. B. *Youth: The years from ten to sixteen.* New York: Harper, 1956.

Glaser, R. Concept learning and concept teaching. In Gagne, R. and Gephart, W. (Eds.), *Learning research and school subjects.* Eighth Annual Phi Delta Kappa Symposium in School Subjects in Educational Research. Itasca, Illinois: F. E. Peacock, 1968.

Gollin, E. S. Organizational characteristics of social judgment: A developmental investigation. *Journal of Personality*, 1958, *26*:139–154.

Goslin, D. A. Accuracy of self-perception and social acceptance. *Sociometry*, 1962, *25*:283–296.

Harvey, O. J., Hunt, D. E., and Schroder, H. M. *Conceptual systems and personality organization.* New York: Wiley, 1961.

Havighurst, R. J., Robinson, M. Z., and Dorr, M. The development of the ideal self in childhood and adolescence. *Journal of Educational Research*, 1946, *40*:241–257.

Heider, F. *The psychology of interpersonal relations.* New York: Wiley, 1958.

Hilgard, E. R. Human motives and the concept of self. *American Psychologist*, 1949, *4*:374–382.

Hollingworth, L. *The psychology of the adolescent.* New York: Appleton-Century-Crofts, 1928.

Homans, G. Human behavior as exchange. *American Journal of Sociology*, 1958, *63*:597–606.

Hooker, D. *The origin of overt behavior.* Ann Arbor: University of Michigan Press, 1944.

Horrocks, J. E. *Assessment of behavior.* Columbus: Merrill, 1964.

Howard, L. P. Identity conflicts in adolescent girls. *Smith College Studies of Social Work*, 1960, *31*:1–21.

Howard, S. M., and Kubis, J. F. Ego identity and some aspects of personal adjustment. *Journal of Psychology*, 1964, *58*:459–466.

Iannaccaro, E. Studio dei modi di reazione alla frustrazione in funzione di certe variabili familari in un gruppo di adolescenti. *Cont. Istit. Psicol.*, 1962, No. *25*:374–387.

Inhelder, B., and Piaget, J. *The growth of logical thinking from childhood to adolescence.* New York: Basic Books, 1958.

Jackson, D. W. Self as process: Implication of role behavior. Unpublished Doctoral Dissertation. Columbus: The Ohio State University, 1970.

James, W. *The principles of psychology* (2 Vol.). New York: Smith, 1890.

Jones, H. E. *Development in adolescence.* New York: Appleton-Century-Crofts, 1943.

Kagan, J., Moss, H. A., and Sigel, I. E. Psychological significance of styles of conceptualization. In Wright, S. C., and Kagan, J. (Eds.) *Monographs of Society for Research in Child Development,* 1963, *28,* No. 2:73–124.

Katz, A., and Zigler, E. Self-image disparity: A developmental approach. *Journal of Personality and Social Psychology,* 1967, *5:*186–195.

Keniston, K. *Young radicals: Notes on committed youth.* New York: Harcourt, Brace & World, 1968.

Kipnis, D. M. Changes in self-concepts in relation to perception of others. *Journal of Personality,* 1961, *29:*449–465.

Kluckhohn, F. R., and Strodtbeck, F. L. *Variations in value orientations.* Evanston, Ill.: Row, Peterson, 1961.

Kohlberg, L. The development of children's orientations toward a moral order. *Vita Humana,* 1963, *6:*11–33.

Kolb, L. C. Disturbances of the body image. In *American Handbook of Psychiatry,* pp. 749–769. New York: Basic Books, 1959.

Kolb, L. C. *The painful phantom.* Springfield, Ill.: Thomas, 1954.

Korzybski, A. The role of language in the perceptual processes. In Blake, R. and Ramsey, G. (Eds.), *Perception: An approach to personality.* New York: Ronald Press, 1951.

Krakovskii, A. P. Psychological bases of an individual approach to the young adolescent. *Doklady Akademii Pedagogicheskikh Nauk RSFSR,* 1962, No. 5.

Krech, D., and Crutchfield, R. S. *Theory and problems of social psychology.* New York: McGraw-Hill, 1948.

Kuhn, M. H. Self-attitudes by age and professional training. *Sociological Quarterly,* 1960, *1:*39–55.

Lane, Robert E. *Political thinking and consciousness.* Chicago: Markham Publishing Company, 1969.

Lecky, P. *Self-consistency: A theory of personality.* New York: Island Press, 1945.

Lewin, K. Comments concerning psychological forces and energies, and the structure of the psyche. Chapter 4 in Rapaport, D. (Ed.), *Organization and pathology of thought.* New York: Columbia University Press, 1951.

Lindbergh, A. M. *Gift from the sea.* New York: Random House, 1955.

Locke, E., and Bryan, J. Cognitive aspects of psychomotor performance: The effects of performance goals on level of performance. *Journal of Applied Psychology,* 1966, *50:*286–291.

Locke, E., and Bryan, J. The effects of goal setting, rule-learning, and knowledge of score on performance. *American Journal of Psychology,* 1966, *79:*451–457.

Lomas, P. Passivity and failure of identity development. *International Journal of Psychology,* 1965, *46:*438–454.

Lunzer, E. A. Problems of formal reasoning in test situations. In Mussen, P. H. (Ed.), European research in cognitive development. *Monographs of the Society for Research in Child Development,* 1965, *30:*19–46.

Macher, M. L., Mensing, J., and Nafzger, S. Concept of self and the reactions of others. *Sociometry,* 1962, *25:*353–357.

Manis, M. Social interaction and the self-concept. *Journal of Abnormal and Social Psychology,* 1955, *51:*362–370.

Manis, M. Personal adjustment: Assumed similarity to parents and inferred parental evaluations of the self. *Journal of Consulting Psychology,* 1958, *22:*481–485.

Martin, W. E. Learning theory and justification: The development of values in children. *Journal of Genetic Psychology,* 1954, *84:*211–217.

Maslow, A. H. *Motivation and personality.* New York: Harper, 1954.

McLuhan, M. *Understanding media: The extension of man.* New York: New American Library, 1964.

Mead, G. H. *Mind, self, and society from the standpoint of a social behaviorist.* (Ed., with introduction, by Charles W. Morris.) Chicago: University of Chicago Press, 1934.

Medinnes, G. R. Adolescents' self-acceptance and perceptions of their parents. *Journal of Consulting Psychology,* 1965, *29:*150–154.

Morris, C. W. (See Mead, G. H.)

Morris, J. F. The development of adolescent value-judgments.

British Journal of Educational Psychology, 1958, *28:* 1–14.

Murphy, G. *Personality*. New York: Harper, 1947.

Murphy, G., and Spohn, H. E. *Encounter with reality*. Boston: Houghton Mifflin, 1968.

Murray, H. A., *et al. Explorations in personality*. New York: Oxford University Press, 1938.

Mussen, P. Some antecedents and consequents of masculine sex-typing in adolescent boys. *Psychological Monographs*, 1961, 75 (Whole No. 506).

Newcomb, T. M. *Social psychology*. New York: Dryden, 1950.

Newcomb, T. M. Persistence and regression of changed attitudes: Long range studies. *Journal of Social Issues*, 1963, *19:*3–14.

Nixon, R. E. An approach to the dynamics of growth in adolescence. *Psychiatry*, 1962, *24:*18–31.

Osgood, C. E., Suci, G. J., and Tannenbaum, P. H. *The measurement of meaning*. Urbana, Ill.: University of Illinois Press, 1957.

Perkins, C. W., and Shannon, D. T. Three techniques for obtaining self-perceptions in pre-adolescent boys. *Journal of Personality and Social Psychology*, 1965, *2:* 443–447.

Piaget, J. *The moral judgment of the child*. London: Kegan Paul, 1932.

Piaget, J. *The psychology of intelligence*. New York: Harcourt, Brace, 1950 (First published in France in 1947).

Piaget, J. *Judgment and reasoning in the child*. New York: Humanities Press, 1952.

Piaget, J. *Six psychological studies*. New York: Random House, 1967.

Pilisuk, M. Cognitive balance and self-relevant attitude. *Journal of Abnormal and Social Psychology*, 1962, *65:*95–103.

Polanyi, M. *Personal knowledge*. Chicago: University of Chicago Press, 1958.

Raup, R. B. *Complacency: The foundation of human behavior*. New York: Macmillan, 1925.

Reese, H. W. Relationship between self-acceptance and sociometric choices. *Journal of Abnormal and Social Psychology*, 1961, *62:*472–474.

Rignano, E. *The psychology of reasoning*. New York: Harcourt, Brace, 1923.

Rivlin, L. G. Creativity and the self-attitudes of sociability of high school students. *Journal of Educational Psychology*, 1959, *50:*147–152.

Rogers, C. R. Some observations on the organization of personality. *American Psychologist*, 1947, *2:*358–368.

Rokeach, M. *The open and closed mind*. New York: Basic Books, 1960.

Rokeach, M. The nature of attitudes. *International Encyclopedia of Social Sciences*. New York: Macmillan, 1968.

Rongved, M. Sex and age differences in self-perception. *Vita Humana*, 1961, *4:*148–158.

Rosen, S., Levinger, G., and Lippitt, R. Desired change in self and others as a function of resource ownership. *Human Relations*, 1960, *13:*187–193.

Rosenberg, M. *Society and the adolescent*. Princeton: Princeton University Press, 1965.

Rotter, J. B. *Social learning and clinical psychology*. New York: Prentice-Hall, 1954.

Rubens, J. L. The self-idealizing and self-alienating process during late adolescence. *American Journal of Psychoanalysis*, 1965, *25:*27–40.

Sanford, N. The development of social responsibility. *American Journal of Orthopsychiatry*, 1967, *37:*22–29.

Sarbin, T. R. Role theory. In Lindzey, G. (Ed.), *Handbook of social psychology*, Vol. 1 Cambridge, Mass.: Addison-Wesley, 1954.

Sarbin, T. R., and Allen, V. L. Role theory. In Lindzey, G., and Aronson, E. (Eds.), *The handbook of social psychology*, Vol. 1. Reading, Mass.: Addison-Wesley, 1968.

Schilder, P. *Image and appearance of the human body: Studies in constructive energies of the psyche*. New York: International Universities Press, 1950.

Schonfeld, W. A. Body image in adolescents: A psychiatric concept for the pediatrician. *Pediatrics*, 1963, *31:*845.

Schur, M. The ego in anxiety. In Loewenstein, R. (Ed.), *Drives, affects, behavior*. New York: International Universities Press, 1953.

Scott, W. A. Cognitive consistency, response reinforcement, and attitude change. *Sociometry*, 1959, 22:219–229.

Scott, W. A. *Values and organizations.* Chicago: Rand McNally, 1965.

Searles, H. F. Concerning the development of an identity. *Psychoanalytic Review*, 1966, 53:7–30.

Sherif, M. The self and reference groups: Meeting grounds of individual and group approaches. *Annals of the New York Academy of Sciences*, 1962, 96 (3):797–813.

Sherif, M., and Cantril, H. *The psychology of ego-involvements.* New York: Wiley, 1947.

Sherrington, C. S. *The brain and its mechanism.* Cambridge: Cambridge University Press, 1933.

Shoben, E. Behavioral aspects of self. *Annals of the New York Academy of Sciences*, 1962, 96:765–773.

Smith, M. B. Personal values and determinants of political attitude. *Journal of Psychology*, 1949, 28:477–486.

Sontag, L. W., and Wallace, R. F. The movement response of the human fetus to sound stimuli. *Child Development*, 1935, 6:253–258.

Sperry, R. W. Neurology and the mind-brain problem. *American Scientist*, 1952, 40:291–312.

Suinn, R. M., and Geiger, J. Stress and the stability of self and other attitudes. *Journal of General Psychology*, 1965, 73:177–180.

Sullivan, H. S. *The interpersonal theory of psychiatry.* New York: Norton, 1953.

Thomas, W., and Znaniecki, F. *The Polish peasant in Europe and America,* (Vol. 1–5). Chicago: University of Chicago Press, 1918.

Turner, R. Role taking, role standpoint and reference group behavior. *American Journal of Sociology*, 1956, *61:* 316–328.

Vygotsky, L. S. *Thought and language.* Cambridge, Mass.: M.I.T. Press, 1962. (This is a translation from the Russian of Vygotsky's book that appeared in 1934.)

Walster, E. The effect of self-esteem on romantic liking. *Journal of Experimental and Social Psychology*, 1965, *1:*184–197.

Weiner, N. *The human use of human beings.* New York: Doubleday, 1954.

Weinstein, E. The development of interpersonal competence. In Goslin, D. A. (Ed.), *Handbook of socialization theory and research.* Chicago: Rand McNally, 1965.

Werdelin, I. Teacher ratings, peer ratings, and self-ratings. *Educational Psychology Inter.*, 1966, *11*:1–19.

Werner, H. *Comparative psychology of mental development.* New York: International Universities Press, 1948.

Wheelis, A. *The quest for identity.* New York: Norton, 1958.

White, R. W. *Lives in progress.* New York: Holt, Rinehart & Winston, 1952.

Witkin, H. A. Origins of cognitive style. In Scheerer, C. (Ed.), *Cognition, theory, research, promise.* New York: Harper & Row, 1964.

Witkin, H. A., Dyk, R. B., Faterson, H. F., Goodenough, D. R., and Karp, S. A. *Psychological differentiation.* New York: Wiley, 1962.

Wohlwill, J. F. A study of the development of the number concept by scalogram analysis. *Journal of Genetic Psychology*, 1960, *96*:347–377.

Wohlwill, J. F., and Lowe, B. C. Experimental analysis of the development of conservation of number. *Child Development*, 1962, *33*:153–167.

Wolberg, L. *The technique of psychotherapy.* New York: Grune and Stratton, 1954.

Wolfe, R. The role of conceptual systems in cognitive functioning at varying levels of age and intelligence. *Journal of Personality*, 1963, *31*:108–123.

Woodruff, A. D., and DiVesta, F. J. The relationship between values, concepts and attitudes. *Educational and Psychological Measurement*, 1948, *8*:645–660.

Wurster, C. R., Bass, B. M., and Alcock, W. We want to be esteemed most by those we esteem most highly. *Journal of Abnormal and Social Psychology*, 1961, *63*:650–653.

Wylie, R. C. *The self-concept.* Lincoln: University of Nebraska Press, 1961.

Yoshikawa, F. Seinenki ni okeru jiga no keisei (Development of self-consciousness in adolescence). *Japanese Journal of Educational Psychology*, 1960, *8*:26–37.

Zachry, C. B., and Lighty, M. *Emotion and conduct in adolescence.* New York: Appleton-Century-Crofts, 1940.

Zazzo, B. L'image de soi comparée à l'image de ses semblables chez l'adolescent. *Enfance,* 1960, No. *2,* 9–141.

Zimbardo, P., and Formica, R. Emotional comparison and self-esteem as determinants of affiliation. *Journal of Personality,* 1963, *31:*141–162

Index